THE FARM

The Farm records the last remnants of a way of life that is dying before our eyes. Richard Benson travels home to Yorkshire to attend the sale of his family's farm. The Bensons have been farming in the county for more than 200 years, but now modern economics have made it impossible for the family to continue. His brother and father must sell what they can and find other ways to earn their living.

Setting the story of the sale, its aftermath and the family's recovery against a background of cataclysmic change in the English countryside, Benson uses memoir, anecdote, reportage and personal insights to explore many social and personal issues: his own disastrous childhood on the farm, his father's sadness, the lost generation of people in his village, and his own attempts to fit in.

The Farm is about childhood, families, change, death, food, alienation and belonging—and about the bond between people and the land and each other.

THE FARM

The Story of One Family and the English Countryside

Richard Benson

WINDSOR
PARAGON

First published 2005
by
Hamish Hamilton
This Large Print edition published 2006
by
BBC Audiobooks Ltd by arrangement with
Penguin Books Ltd

Hardcover ISBN 10: 1 4056 1557 5
           ISBN 13: 978 1 405 61557 0
Softcover ISBN 10: 1 4056 1558 3
           ISBN 13: 978 1 405 61558 7

British Library Cataloguing in Publication Data available

C46086121/

Printed and bound in Great Britain by
Antony Rowe Ltd., Chippenham, Wiltshire

This book is for my family,

and in memory of Jessie, 1932-2003

Author's Note and Acknowledgements

Some of the names of people and places in this book have been changed. More information can be found at www.thefarm.uk.com

I'd like to thank David Godwin and Simon Prosser for their support and encouragement; Julian Rudd for his wisdom and patience; Laura for her advice and understanding. Also Stephen Armstrong, Ted Atkinson, Cally Barker, Ian Bell, Jane Birdsell, James Bolton, John and Sheila Bowers, John and Jim Coleman, Gareth Coombes, Helma Craik, John Edmondson, Ekow Eshun, Kevin Foord, Louise France and Roger Alton, Prue Jeffreys, John and Sue Johnston, Jennifer Kabat, Robin Maynard, Juliette Mitchell, Sean Moore, Johnny Myers, Steve Petch, Miranda Sawyer, JRS, Kevin Welsh and Nina Whitby.

I give a false name and address when I sign for the keys.

It is five o'clock on a late December night, already dark. The estate agent's office has a Christmas tree in the corner and blinking lights Blutacked around the windows.

'London,' says the woman behind the desk, looking at the address I have written in the log book. 'We get ever so many up from London now. We seem to be the in place!'

'Oh,' I say.

'Must be t' fresh air.' She is making me a bit nervous with her talking. Someone might come in and recognize me, so I want to get out of the office. She pushes the keys across the desk and smiles. 'Let us know what you think tomorrow, if you can.'

I drive back out to our village and up to the caravan in the spinney to collect my dad.

*   *   *

The house that my dad and I have come to view is a newly converted barn, huddled with other converted farm buildings around a small gravelled courtyard in our village. We are standing outside its large, stable-style front door, me untangling the knot of keys lent by the estate agent, and my dad warily eyeing the one house in the courtyard with lights on. He is worried about being seen here. I have persuaded him to accompany me by promising that at this hour the neighbours would still be at work.

1

Now, in the shadows thrown by the far porchlight, both his complaisance and his curiosity about the barn's damp-proofing are yielding to doubt.

'Mebbe tha's got t' wrong keys,' he whispers.

'It says "barn" on the tag.'

'Try turning t' handle t' other way then.'

The doors swing open. Nervously we step in, close the doors behind us, and turn on the lights. The decor is fussily mock-rustic: low, beamed ceilings, exposed chalk and brick walls, pastel flowers painted on every available surface. In the lavatory by the front door, the toilet bowl and cistern are decorated with pastel, willow-pattern prints. In the farmhouse-style kitchen along the hall, some of the ceramic tiles are in the form of pastel-painted bas-relief fruits—a feature which seems to impress my dad, who is looking bemused.

'Fancy, in't it?' he whispers, gingerly prodding at a pale-green ceramic pear.

'I suppose so,' I say.

We are both uneasy. Running his hand along a beam, my dad observes that the ceiling seems very low and then, stepping backwards, he bangs his head against a glass lampshade decorated with primroses. The shade swings violently. 'I'm scared I'm going to break summat,' he says, reaching out to steady it. 'Let's have a look at that wall instead.'

He steps up to the exposed chalk wall and runs his fingertips over the stones, squinting in contemplation.

'I don't understand this leaving chalk and brick bare. Not in houses.'

'I think it's fashionable.'

'I know it's fashionable, I've seen it on telly,' he says. 'But to me it looks mucky. If I were buying a

new house I'd want it to look clean.'

He rubs at the patches of salt crystals sprouting where dampness has come through the rock. 'Tha sees, I thought they'd have trouble damp-proofing t' chalk. Chalk loves water, and water's its own master . . . What's tha looking at?'

I have found, at head-height on the far side of the room, a pair of the eighteen-inch slits that once provided the building's light and ventilation. The slits have been covered with a pane of glass decorated with an oddly-shaped sea creature. I am remembering one summer, many years ago now, working in shafts of sunlight shining through them.

'I'm just looking at that . . . dolphin.'

'Oh,' he says, walking over. 'I thought it were a fish.'

'It could well be a fish.'

We stand side by side, considering the dolphin-fish. Outside in the courtyard, kitchen lights are going on.

My dad watches a car pulling up outside the house opposite. 'We'd better be getting on—'

'How do you feel being here, Dad?' I blurt out.

He doesn't say anything.

'I just meant . . . does it bother you?'

He looks down and sighs. 'It's hard to say, lad, I—'

Suddenly there is a knock at the front door. The latch lifts. My dad ducks out of view.

'Hello?' A woman's voice curls in round the door.

'Hi!' I call back, casually jogging back down the hall.

'Can I help you at all?' The woman is in her fifties, with short grey hair, gold jewellery, and rather

3

hawklike eyes. She is very obviously trying to memorize my appearance in case she is later called upon to describe me to a police officer.

'I'm just viewing,' I say. 'I got the keys from the estate agent.' To emphasize this, I hold them up in front of her.

'Oh! Right—right,' she says. She looks slightly disappointed. 'I live across there, and just saw the lights on, you know.'

'It's good to know people keep a look out.'

'Have to, these days.' The woman shows no interest in leaving. Folding her arms under her bosom, and leaning against the lavatory door jamb, she seems to be settling in for a chat. 'Have you come far?'

'London. Grew up here, but thinking of coming back.'

'Oh, I'm an out-of-towner myself. Leeds. We've been here a year and a bit.' She says 'a year and a bit' as if it were half a lifetime.

'Right.'

She smiles and nods.

'Do you like it here?'

'Ooh, smashing. This courtyard's so quiet, you can go all day without seeing a soul.'

'Sounds lovely.'

'It used to be a farmyard, you know.'

'Yes,' I said. 'I know.'

Pig Trouble

This story really begins five years earlier, on a windy, rain-blackened day in September. It was half past eight in the morning, and I was in the kitchen of my flat in London getting ready to go to work when my dad rang.

'Eyup lad,' he said. 'Has tha got a minute?'

'Oh, hello Dad!' I was surprised to hear from him, because at half past eight in the morning he and my brother were usually in their yard, feeding pigs. 'Are you all right?'

He took a deep breath, and when he spoke he sounded phlegmy and distant. 'Um, Richard. Me and thy mam's got a bit of bad news for thee.'

I picked up the TV remote control, and popped off the BBC *Breakfast* news. There was a moment of silence. I remembered my brother muttering gloomily about money in our last conversation, on the phone about four months ago.

'We've had a visit from t' bank manager,' said my dad. 'He says we've to sell up and get some debts paid off or else we'll lose t' house.'

'Do you mean all the pigs?' I was trying to help him avoid having to say it, but instead I threw him off course.

'Oh—nay, nay lad,' he said. 'It's all t' lot. Pigs, and t' yard and t' lot, like. We've rung t' auctioneer and he says he can do t' sale on t' thirty-first of October.'

That was in six weeks' time. 'Like an auction?' I asked. 'It doesn't seem very long.'

'Aye, a farm sale, tha knows. Bank manager says

5

we've to get on wi' it. Jim Croskill's lending us a field to put t' tackle in.'

'I'll come and help you.'

He did not reply to this.

'I'll come up tomorrow.'

'Not if tha's busy, lad. There's nowt tha can do—'

'I know, but—'

'I didn't mean . . .'

'I know. I just want to come and see you and Mum.'

'Aye, well—'

'And our Guy.'

'Aye . . .' He sighed. 'He's said nowt about it, Guy.'

'I suppose he never says much about anything, does he?'

'Nay, but I used to . . . I never know what he thinks now. He'll mebbe say summat to thee if tha comes, eh?'

'Yeah, maybe.'

There was another silence, longer than the last. My dad's breathing wavered and roughened. I said, 'I'm sure it'll be OK, Dad—'

But awkwardly he cut in, spilling words: 'Thy mam an't taken it very good, I think she'd like to see thee—' And then his voice died away into a small, spittly choke.

I had never heard him sound like this before. Some facts about my father: he is six foot one, with a 52-inch chest and the heft of a heavyweight boxer. Once when I was a child I stood in a potato field and watched the David Brown forage harvester, under which he was lying while trying to clean its blades, slip off its jack and fall so its tow

6

bar smashed into his right shin and broke it in three places. He cursed once, then pulled his leg clear, hobbled to his van and drove himself to the doctor's surgery. Dr Clough cut off the torn wellington boot, looked impassively at the broken leg and said, in the same resigned tone of voice he used for predicting poor results for the Yorkshire cricket team, 'Looks like a hospital job, Gordon. Can Pauline drive you? She'll be quicker than the ambulance.'

My dad's voice in the receiver snapped me back into the present. '. . . but we'd all like to see thee, tha knows that.'

'Right. I'll come,' I said. 'I'll get a train tomorrow.'

I put the handset back in its cradle and stood still, listening blankly to the burr of the fridge, the thrumming of the rain and the distant engines of the school-run traffic. I imagined my dad two hundred miles away, walking across the flagstone hallway and into the kitchen where my mum would be making coffee, and Guy sitting stroking a cat and saying nowt about anything.

Twenty minutes later, I took the bus to my office. I worked as an editor at a small magazine publishing company, and that morning I had a breakfast meeting with the other editors and the advertising sales staff. When I slipped into the exposed-brick and glass meeting room fifteen minutes late, I caught a flak of small sighs and glares from my colleagues. I found it hard to concentrate in the meeting, and contributed very little, despite the continuing pointed looks over the cafetière.

Guy

Amid the swarming, clattering travellers, Great North Eastern Railway staff and trolleys piled high with suitcases, I saw the thick, dark eyebrows of my brother Guy lift by approximately one millimetre in greeting as I came down the steps of the footbridge at York railway station. Guy speaks like most men in the village we come from, i.e. not at all until he has spent five minutes considering whether there are other means of communication he can use instead. His favourites are the eyebrow-raise, the shrug, and the brief lift of his chin; if he is feeling particularly emotional, he may perform all three together. That morning, as I worked my bags through the crowds, he kept his eyebrows raised. Standing in his work clothes, he resembled a large, solitary rusty nail: his steel-capped boots, battered, formless waxed jacket and heavy stubble seemed to be causing many people to give him a wide berth.

'Hello, Guy,' I said.

'Now then,' he replied. 'Give us one of your bags.'

'Thank you,' I said, and passed him a holdall.

'Fucking hell! What the fuck have you got in here?'

My brother is appalled by indulgences such as luggage, although his exclamations are less aggressive than resignedly bemused. With Guy, you have to understand that when he asks what the fuck you've got in a bag, it is a way of saying, 'Hello, how are you?' You also have to get used to

8

the way he uses the word 'fuck' all the time, except in front of our mother.

'It'll be the computer that's heavy. And there's some books.'

'Books,' he said wearily, shaking his head. 'Fucking hell.'

'Sorry.'

'Dun't matter,' he said. 'It's not that heavy.' He yanked the bag up on to his shoulder.

'It's nice to see you, Guy.'

Guy raised his eyebrows and chin five millimetres, and strode off towards the car park.

I felt relieved by his distracted, unemotional expression because it was usual: since he was a small child he had gone through much of life looking as if he was pondering the answer to a complex mathematical problem. But as I caught up with him and looked at him from the side, I noticed dark half-circles below his eyes.

'Are you all right, then?' I said.

He raised his eyebrows again, and blew out through pursed lips. He looked as if he were trying to pop the features off his face. Then he gave me the sort of consolation smile you give relatives whose partners have left them, batted his lashy black-brown eyes and shrugged.

'You look a bit tired,' I said.

'I should think I fucking do,' he said. 'Been doing twelve-hour days since July. Any road, I see hairdresser's scissors are still on ration in London.'

My hair, which is only collar-length, is regarded as another indulgence by Guy, who keeps his hair at a tidy inch. I tried to think of something funny to say in reply, but I couldn't, and he wasn't interested anyway. He concentrated on opening

9

the back door of his old green rusting Diahatsu Fourtrak without anything falling out.

'Sling your bags in t' back, then,' he said breezily.

Slinging my bags into the back of Guy's truck was not as straightforward as he made it sound. He used it as a combined workshop, storage unit and mobile home, and so as well as the usual driving-dregs of pasty wrappers, plastic bottles and broken CD cases, there was farm equipment of an often surprising scale—straw bales, black five-gallon polythene barrels, cardboard boxes for the transport of piglets, bundles of shovels and muck-forks, metal toolboxes which were themselves the size of small cars, and modern tools which I did not recognize or understand. Intermingled with that was random, inexplicable household bric-a-brac: sofa cushions, an Aiwa stereo speaker, half a dozen plant pots, several caps, two garden fence posts, a small roll of carpet and a blanket coated with cat hairs. Sometimes the farm cats jumped in there when he opened the back door in the morning, and if he drove off somewhere they stayed unnoticed, dozing a day away between map books, buckets and muck-forks. Occasionally, when one quick pint in town became several, he climbed in and slept there himself.

I gingerly balanced the bags on some barrels, and then walked round the truck and climbed into the front passenger seat. When Guy got in and slammed his door, I heard my bags falling off into the plant pots.

'I thought they'd tumble off there,' he said.

I looked down at the dusty passenger dashboard, which handled the spillover from the

10

back: pliers, notebooks, tape measures, Coke cans, a mobile phone in a case wreathed with mud and straw.

Guy stamped down the accelerator and we shot out of the pay-and-display car park and across the taxi rank. As he steered the Fourtrak's nose into the city traffic, he grinned a gallows grin, leaned forward to see the oncoming cars, and said, 'A' course this is all your fault, you know.'

Sowthistle

'Funny,' I said, and Guy looked ahead into the traffic, lifted his eyebrows and moved his mouth in what may or may not have been a grin. As we drove around the medieval city walls I watched his face to try to catch his expression when the half-grin lapsed, but he just lost himself in nonchalant concentration on the other cars and vans around us. For something to do, I turned on the radio-cassette and began retuning it to Radio 5. This caused a very loud static noise to fill the cab, and Guy to jerk round in his seat, shouting, 'DON'T TOUCH THAT RADI—'

I snapped it off, and looked at him again. 'Sorry.'

'Never mind,' he said. He gritted his teeth, and we drove in silence for a few seconds.

'It only plays Radio 1, and it takes me ages to get that.' I could tell he was annoyed because he wasn't swearing.

'Sorry,' I said again.

He looked at me, then back out of the

windscreen, and blinked slowly. 'I usually listen to that,' he said, glancing down at a Sony Discman that was stuck to the dashboard top with yellow insulating tape. It was lightly coated with dried mud, and wired up to the radio-cassette. 'CDs are in t' glove compartment.'

There were seven CDs, all albums by Sheryl Crow. Last Christmas, while trying to make conversation in the village pub, I had asked Guy to name his top ten albums of all time. He said he couldn't understand why I was always making lists like that, and then named five, all of which were by Sheryl Crow.

I put on *Tuesday Night Music Club*, but because my brother and the Discman's anti-skip mechanism had given up on each other, the songs were punctuated by random five-second silences. Guy, tapping the steering wheel in time with the music, seemed quite content with this. When the CD stopped his fingers hovered above the steering wheel, and then resumed tapping when it started again. As we accelerated off at the bypass roundabout the music was drowned out by the engine noise anyway. We left Sheryl Crow on the A64 walking off towards Santa Monica Boulevard, and we didn't say anything any more to each other as we splashed first across the flat, wet Vale of York, and then suddenly, steeply, up through low clouds on to the hills of the Yorkshire Wolds.

It takes only twenty minutes to drive through the hills, scarps and slacks between the Wolds' western shoulder and our village, but that day the journey seemed to take hours. Neither of us could think of anything to say to each other, so Guy pretended to concentrate on his windscreen-wiper speeds, and I leant my forehead against the side window and looked out.

As we came over the top of the hill overlooking our village the country opened up below us: broad chalk valleys, scattered conifer plantations and, on a low ridge, the place where we had grown up: Sowthistle. Sowthistle is a practical, working English village built mostly of brick and pantile, with a few old walls of greenish-white chalk. At its centre a Norman church tower rises out of black yews and elms; around that is a functional jumble of houses and cottages, farmyards, a school, two pubs, a pond, a post office and an angular, modern Methodist chapel. In the fields around it are outlying farms, tied cottages, a small sewage works and a disused railway station. On the northern horizon stands a vast monument, built in 1866 to honour Chester Skelton, a baronet whose family enclosed and developed thirty thousand acres of Wolds land. The monument has the effect of calling the landscape into order around itself, but it is an unlovely structure which from a distance resembles a Victorian Gothic space rocket.

As we drove through the village I noticed three of the small farms on the main street had For Sale notices outside, and two had builders in their yards. One farmer had converted his sprouts shed into an antiques shop. A house opposite the chapel had a bed-and-breakfast sign in the window.

We turned off the main road into a narrow lane between Bob Batty's chalk-and-brick barns and the churchyard. Rose Farm, our home, was along the lane. As we drove into the farmyard, the Fourtrak's broad tyres splashing up mud, stones and rainwater puddles, the pigs in sties and pens

13

around us stirred, looked up, and sniffed; as we got out of the truck, most heaved themselves to their feet and slowly lumbered up to their gates. Guy rubbed their snouts, and I levered one of my bags out from where it had become lodged, upside-down, between a jerrycan and a toolbox. From back up the lane I heard the sounds of hammers, cement mixers and scraping shovels.

'Is Bob building on his yard?' I asked Guy, surprised.

'Bob's packed up,' he said, slamming the Fourtrak's door with a force that made the watching pigs blink. 'Skeltons sold t' yard for building houses on and took his land back for Highthorpe Estate.'

'What's Bob doing?'

'He retired. They've moved to Kirksfield cos Christine wanted to live in a town. Nobody would've wanted t' farm, like, cos it's too small.'

'I thought Bob's farm was big.' Bob Batty's was the old Manor Farm, owned by the Skeltons, whose estate was based in the village of Highthorpe, up near the monument.

'It was, but size of everything's changed, like. Three hundred acres isn't big any more.'

'Oh.'

'It's not like when you lived here, you know.'

'I can see that,' I said.

Two Pairs of Boots

I cleaned my shoes on the boot-scraper near the hollow stone doorstep, opened the door, and dropped my bags in the hallway.

In the kitchen my mum and dad were sitting in their usual places at the table: Dad in the far corner with his strawy-socked feet stretched out, and a good view of the portable telly, Mum at his side within an arm's reach of the cluttered worktop and geriatric pale-blue Aga. They were eating their midday meal, which they called dinner, ours being a dinner-and-tea rather than lunch-and-supper family: breadcakes from the baker's van, thick-cut cold bacon and beef from the butcher's in Kirksfield, a pork pie, a two-pint jar of home-made piccalilli and a bowl of silvery-mauve damsons that would most likely be a gift from a friend in the village. Around their legs the two black farm cats miaowed for bits of meat, and my mum's pet rabbit, a large tawny-coloured English lop called Peter, gnawed a cabbage leaf. As Guy and I sat down in our old places, a cat cuffed Peter on the jaw, and the rabbit scuttled past me towards a corner, where he began sniffing at a tatty carrier bag full of pears.

'What you been doing at work, lad?' asked my mum.

I said I had been writing cover lines for a magazine cover with Chris Evans on the front.

'Him with the glasses?' she said. 'I think he's touched!'

My mum often says things which, especially if

15

you write them down, sound quite eccentric. But she's not really eccentric, just sort of bluntly, innocently forthright. She also combines a live-and-let-live philosophy with the conviction that most people on television are borderline insane.

'I didn't know Bob had sold up,' I said.

'Oh aye,' said my dad. 'They all are, like. They're building no end of houses. They all seem to be wanting to come to villages.'

I noticed that on the calendar under the white plastic wall clock, in the space for last Wednesday, my mum had written in blue ballpoint capitals: BANK.

No one seemed ready to mention the sale. I asked if they'd seen the auctioneer, but my dad just mumbled something about him coming next week, and then they didn't speak for a bit. My mum looked out of the window, and my dad looked down at his hands on the table.

'Manager came from t' bank, Richard,' said my mum, turning back. 'He had a little computer, and he put it on t' table and showed us all t' money. We were spending less fattening 'em than we were ten years since, but we were losing between ten and thirteen pound for every pig that we sold.'

'Nobody wants pigs at all,' said my dad. 'Nobody'll even come and fetch 'em. And it's no good carrying on, 'cause most people say it'll get worse, and t' bank manager'll not guarantee any more cheques. Overdraft's as much as t' yard's worth, tha sees. If we carry on, we'll lose t' house. They reckon even Gerald Thwaites is struggling.'

Gerald Thwaites owned a very large farm in Ullestoft, a village to the south of Sowthistle.

'Why, though? Surely if they took them to

16

market, somebody would buy them just because they were cheap?'

Guy turned away from the conversation.

'There are hardly any markets any more. Most little ones've shut. It's all big food companies that buys stuff, and they want big producers who can give 'em a constant supply that's always t' same. Buying's in that few hands, they can more or less control t' prices, and if it does go over a certain price, they just get on t' phone and bring it in from abroad.'

'Everybody goes on about fresh food and free-range pork and all that,' said Guy, looking at me as if I was the president of the Free-range Pork Society, 'but if they can get it fucking cheaper—'

'Language, Guy,' said my mum, and Guy looked away again, glowering.

'You don't know what you're buying now,' she said to me. 'They buy pigs from Poland and process them at Winterswick bacon factory, and then put on t' label that it's British cured. You buy York ham at t' supermarket, and it's never been anywhere near York.'

'Maybe you could complain to the supermarket,' I said hopefully.

'I did! I had a conversation about meat with a man on t' meat counter in Kwik Save, but he said it's what people want. I said, "Well, I'm a person and I don't want it," but he just laughed. I don't know who "people" are supposed to be.'

Guy studiously dropped white ham fat into the cats' paws, and the rabbit inched back from its corner. Suddenly a white, silky newborn piglet tumbled out of the bottom oven of the Aga, and sat blinking on the carpet. In cold weather, my dad

17

and Guy wrapped weak piglets in old tea towels, and laid them in the oven to keep warm. This usually provided some entertainment for the cats and rabbit, who were now all sniffing at the pig as it tried to push itself up on its thin, quivering legs.

'It in't just us, like,' said my dad. No one took any notice of the piglet. 'There's a lot lost their houses, and you see all t' blokes working for 'em that live in tied houses, same like. At least if we pack up now we'll have somewhere to live.'

'We didn't fancy camping,' said Mum.

'It all just seems terrible,' I said limply.

Guy snorted. 'It's more than fucking terrible—'

'Guy!' shouted Mum.

'Sorry!' he shouted back. Scowling, he threw his last fat scrap on to a cat's head. 'Have we to get going again?' he asked Dad.

'Aye, fetch us me boots then.'

Guy went into the hallway and brought back their lace-up work boots. This was a little ritual. They always left their boots in the hallway at mealtimes, out of respect for the kitchen carpet. However, after the meal one of them fetched the boots into the kitchen, so that they could both put them on while finishing off their second mugs of tea. Flakes and rinds of mud got left on the carpet, but my mum seemed satisfied with the gesture.

In the hall Guy picked up a pair of green overalls and stepped into them, and my dad put on his faded blue smock jacket. Then they took their caps, oily and frayed, inner rims blackened by dirt and sweat, and pulled them down on their heads tightly in anticipation of the rain outside.

'What you doing this afternoon?' said my mum, clearing the table.

18

'Finding a bank to rob,' said my dad, coming back into the kitchen to collect the piglet.

'Don't forget your gun.'

'Aye. Make us a cup of tea for about four o'clock, will tha?'

Guy opened the door and strode out into the hissing rain. My dad, with the tiny pig under one arm and his shoulders rolling unevenly because of his right-leg limp, followed.

'Bloody hell, it's a wet 'un today, lad!' I heard my dad say in admiring tones. When I left Sowthistle, he and my brother had yet to see the weather condition that did not merit exclamation or debate; this, at least, appeared to be unchanged.

'Oh aye!' enthused Guy. 'It's a bastard!'

You were allowed to swear when you got out of the house, but today my mum didn't seem to be listening anyway.

Skills

My mum washed the pots, and I stood beside her, drying.

'What a going-on,' she said.

'It'll be OK, Mum.'

'Did our Guy say owt to you when you came? He's hardly talked to me and your dad. We don't know if he's keeping it all in or what.'

'Not really,' I said. 'I asked him but he just sort of laughed it off.'

'He's tired out. He's been working for Jim Croskill to earn a bit of money, and then coming home and starting with your dad. They've not been

19

coming in while nine and ten o'clock, and they're both worn out. They put brave faces on, but—' She bit her lips together to stop tears coming. 'I don't know what we're going to do, Richard.' Her hands fished for knives and forks in the water. 'I mean I can't think what we'll live on.'

'Come on, Mum—' I said. I put my arm around her shoulders and she turned and hugged me. Still holding the tea towel in one hand, I hugged her back. She felt small in my arms, and I felt the warm soapsuds from her hands seeping wet through my shirt and jumper. 'Try not to worry, I'm sure it'll be all right.'

'What will we live on, though? Who wants such as me and your dad for work? We've no skills or qualifications or—'

'You have got skills. You and my dad can do all sorts.'

'Not skilled things,' she said. 'I don't even know how to turn a computer on.'

'There are more skills than using computers, Mum.'

'They always want you to use computers, though. I went to have a look in t' jobcentre when I went to do my shopping, and all t' adverts said computers—I didn't even know what they meant.'

Thinking about the jobcentre made her cry again, and as the cement mixers across in Bob Batty's yard rumbled on in the background, we both stood there wondering what was going to happen.

She backed out of my arms, pulled a small cotton hanky from a sleeve and wiped her eyes. 'I'm sorry, lad, we didn't want to depress you as well. Look, do you want this jar of piccalilli?'

'Maybe I'll take it back another time,' I said. 'Is our Helen coming?'

'She came yesterday, but she had to go back to Hull. She says she'll come next weekend. I bet you're busy at work as well.'

'Well, it doesn't matter. It's only Chris Evans.'

'Well, if it's only him—'

'Exactly.'

'He hasn't got skills has he?'

'Not very useful ones.'

She stacked the plates in a corner cupboard which also contained a shotgun, pig medications and some small bottles of certified boar sperm, then sat down at the table.

'I just can't think what we'll do,' she said. 'Me and your dad, we don't know anything else.'

Mal

The small brick outhouse by the back door of Rose Farm contained the overspills of farmyard and kitchen. In the corner opposite the door sat Peter's home-made, kennel-sized hutch, and from the roofbeams above, bunches of carrots and onions hung down like rabbit dreams. In every other available space bulky work coats, boots and hats were stacked and stuffed between sacks of potatoes, offcuts of wood, tractor parts and sundry broken tools awaiting repair.

On the Saturday morning after I arrived home, I loitered there sheepishly as my dad looked through a box of mismatched, cobwebby footwear for me. Having forgotten to pack any work clothes

21

I had had to borrow some of his old ones, and now stood in a pair of sagging brown corduroy trousers and a pink check shirt with its collar hanging off.

'There's a pair of my old boots here, looks tha—' He yanked from a small heap of creased, busted and dusty boots a pair of short, black Argyll wellingtons that belched dust as he stood them on the floor. One of them was kinked, and it fell over.

'And a coat up theer if tha's cold.' He looked towards a patched and fraying ex-army greatcoat hanging on a peg on the wall. I remembered the coat being there when I was at school, and I suspected that no one had removed it from its peg for at least twenty years.

My mum came in with a small bowlful of cabbage leaves and Honey Nut Loops for Peter's breakfast.

'Now then, lad,' she said to the rabbit, as she inserted Honey Nut Loops through the wire of his hutch. 'Do you want to come in this morning, or are you staying there?'

'That rabbit gets treated better than we do, tha knows,' my dad said to me.

'Because he gives me less gyp,' Mum said, looking back over her shoulder. 'You want to take them clothes back to London with you and start a fashion, Richard. People are daft enough.'

The rain had stopped, but in the yard the gutters were dripping and drains sluicing, and a bad-tempered wind banged unlatched doors against walls. As the pigs heard us coming down the short path from the house, they began jostling each other and shrieking. We rushed to feed the biggest pen—the foldyard in the middle of the horseshoe-shaped shanty town of sheds—first.

22

This killed off the worst of the noise, and as we splashed around the yard feeding the rest, the shrieking gradually calmed to a strawy, munching quiet. When we finished, my dad and Guy went to sort out the sows that were due to pig, and left me to muck out the weaners.

My dad always kept his pigs on straw, although it had long been popular to use simple concrete or wooden slats instead. There was less work in keeping wood and concrete clean, and cleanliness meant less risk of disease, but he stuck with straw: he thought you got better, happier pigs on it. When I lived at home he cleaned them out every Friday, dumping the wet, black straw on a vast steaming muck-hill that rotted through the year, and was spread over the fields in winter. This free fertilizer was useful, but it did entail a lot of labour. Pigs are clean animals, and a group generally defecates close to where they get their water and leaves the rest of the pen dry for sleeping in. However, a leaking pipe or an unpredictable decision to reverse the usual toilet arrangements can lead to dirty straw in the sleeping area, and so, several times through the week, someone had to check the sties and shovel any wet straw outside.

I began that morning's check in the old brick-and-chalk barn with the wall-slits. Inside was a haystack, a hen loft and sties with low, covered-over backs. The sties were dimly lit by single light bulbs caked in fly eggs and laced with cobwebs, and the whole building felt warm and dusky. Maybe it was the darkness, but as I got down on my knees to rake out the wet straw I began to feel strangely peaceful. So I was quite startled when

23

something rustled outside the sty, and moved into the light behind me.

'Knee-deep in shit again, lad,' it said.

I first made out a pair of thick spectacle lenses, and then some teeth in a gingery beard, so that for a moment it was as if the gloom above me had grown a talking face. Then the green overalls straining across the chest, the cowlick of dark hair across the wide white forehead, and finally the face's expression—a blend of despondency and kindness that had always reminded me of a lone raindrop slipping down a window-pane.

'Hello, Mal,' I said.

'Bet tha thought tha'd finished wi' this fucking caper,' said the face, disappearing back into the dark to look for some straw.

'You could say that.' This was always a useful answer when you didn't know quite what to say.

'Aye. I reckon tha had t' right idea in t' end.'

'Maybe.'

'Fucking definitely.'

Mal reappeared with some clean straw torn from a bale, and threw it into the back for me. I scattered it about, and let myself out of the sty.

'Are you all right, then?' I asked.

'What, me?' he said, as if I might have been trying to strike up conversation with a pig. 'Strugglin' on, I suppose.'

Malcolm Garside is my dad's friend. He rents from the County Council a 200-acre farm that his father had before him, and has worked at it with grim concentration since he left Sowthistle School at the age of fifteen. Mal became a village legend in the early 1980s after his fight with his bull, a 750-kilo Friesian that he kept in a field near his

24

yard. The bull had knocked him down, tossed him six feet in the air, and was kneeling down to pummel him with its head when Mal, realizing that he had landed near the fence, rolled under the lower rail and escaped. Clutching at broken ribs, not yet aware of his damaged back muscles, he walked down to his yard, collected a headless axe shaft, and went back to the field to resume the fight. It was months before he could lift heavy weights again, but he kept the bull until, years later, he took Government money to sell off the milk herd he and his dad had built up. 'No point,' he told me when, in my early teens, I asked if he wasn't worried about the bull attacking again. 'Tha can never be sure of any of 'em—bulls, boars, stallions, they're all t' same. Same as most blokes can be if they're that way out.'

Mal believed that everything would go wrong or disappoint you in the end, was possessed by a pessimism so deep and constant it gave him a sort of transcendence. Even in the hottest days of high summer, when the smiling television weather girls were slapping down yellow sun stickers in the morning forecasts, he would be deciding what to do when the rain came. And as the rain always did come, who could ever say he was wrong? When I was growing up, I used to get a lot of comfort from talking to Mal.

Now we walked up the yard together, looking for my dad. 'I don't know what to say, Mal. I don't know what to make of any of it,' I said.

He said that he didn't know either, and he didn't know what would happen to old buggers like him and my dad, because what else could they do? He told me that with his two daughters left home,

25

his wife Eileen had started going to line-dancing classes that some new bloke in the village had started doing in the village hall. Eileen and Mal had been married for about thirty years. She worked with him on the farm; on their wedding day, Mal had driven her to the Grand Hotel in Scarborough for tea, then back home again for milking, and that had been the honeymoon.

'Don't you fancy line dancing?' I asked him. He turned his head about five degrees and grimaced.

My mum was feeding the rest of the cabbage leaves to the pigs in the foldyard. 'Now then, Pauline,' he said.

'Eyup, Mal—you all right?'

'Strugglin' on,' he said. 'Back's a bit bad. I'm getting bloody old is what it is.'

'How's your Eileen? Is she still into t' line dancing?'

'Oh, bloody hell, aye,' he replied, shaking his head.

'You want to get yourself off with her. A bit of dancing'd do you good.'

'I don't think I'll be dancing in this lifetime lass . . .' Then, turning to me, he said, 'Tha likes going out . . . ravin' dun't tha?'

'Well, now and again,' I said.

'Is tha going out in Kirksfield t'neet then?' He shook his head again forebodingly at the thought of Saturday night in our local town.

'I should think so. With Guy, maybe.'

'On thy own head be it,' he said.

You Get Very Philosophical Out Ploughing on Your Own All Day

Kirksfield is seven miles from Sowthistle, and sits down on the flat, fieldy plain between the Wolds and the North Sea. Despite Mal's opinion of its nightlife, it is like most other Yorkshire market towns, with a street of local shops in the middle, a light industrial estate on the outskirts, and a market square with a clock that is usually wrong. At nine o'clock on Saturday evening Guy and I got out of a minicab and walked across the market square where men were shouting instructions to each other about which pub they were going to, and women were linking arms laughing.

'You meeting a lady, then?' I asked. I was trying to generate a sort of knockabout, brotherly tone to take Guy's mind off things.

'No,' he said.

'What happened to Mandy?' Mandy was a girl from Kirksfield who worked behind the bar in the Black Bull. At Christmas, Guy had been going out with her and seemed quite keen.

'She went on about me having to work all t' time. We were building some new pig sheds and I hadn't seen her much. One night she was working behind t' bar and says to everybody, "Oh, he's more bothered about his shed than he is about me." But we had to get 'em up before it got wet.'

'Couldn't you have explained to her?'

'I tried, but to be honest, I did think more about my shed,' he said. 'She was nice, but I knew it wasn't to be.'

27

As we passed the clock, which had a range of times on its four faces, a group of laughing girls in stilettos clacked and teetered past. I suggested that one of them had been eyeing Guy up, which made him sigh. 'I never seem to meet anyone in Kirksfield. There's somebody, maybe, but— sometimes when I'm feeling down about it, it seems like all . . . druggies and bench wenches. I mean obviously that's not *everyone*, but—'

'Hang on, what's a bench wench?'

'A wench who sits on a bench,' he said. 'Like them.' He looked over at another group of girls milling about some cast-iron seats in the square.

'Mandy went weird, you know,' he said. 'I found her one night kicking the wheels of my truck. And she put this anti-GM foods sticker in t' back window of her car cos she thought it'd piss me off. As if everybody who works on a farm's into GM food.'

'Aren't they?'

'Some are, some aren't,' he said. 'It depends on the person. If they've got shares in a large seed company, I imagine they'll be very keen.'

We headed to a pub called the Viking, part of a multi-purpose development called the Norseman Centre which was built in the Eighties by a local businessman trying to exploit interest in the area's Viking heritage. The centre had in the past included Odin's Bar, Thor's Nightclub, the Saxon Lounge and the Valkyrie Gym. It now also had the Valhalla Nightclub where Guy worked odd nights as a bouncer.

A roar of heat and noise blasted us as we pushed through double doors. I found a wonky table in a corner, and Guy brought over two pints of Beck's which slopped over on to the carpet when he put them down.

'Is there a lot of people taking drugs then?' I asked, scraping the lager off the table with a beer mat. When I was growing up in Kirksfield in the early 1980s, most casual drug use in the town had been limited to smoking cannabis and eating magic mushrooms. If adults talked about drugs at all, they talked as if they were something that happened somewhere else.

'I'd say a fair few. E, but more dope, and then heroin with a few of 'em. I think that's why there's more thieving. I have to cover my tools up if I park in Kirksfield now, like. Nicking tools is a big thing.'

'Why, do you think?'

'Cos tools are valuable.'

'I meant, why do you think more people take drugs?'

'They say boredom, and people from Hull coming out to sell 'em—but I don't know. It's just the same as going out and getting pissed, but more fashionable, and it's not frowned on like getting pissed. Being an alcoholic's unacceptable, but if you're hooked on drugs it's supposed to make you interesting. Do you remember Maxine English?'

Maxine English was a robust blonde woman who ran the bar in the White Horse at the top of the town. It was rumoured that she had had sex with all seven members of Showaddywaddy on the night they played Bridlington Spa Hall in 1978.

'They reckon her and her daughter are dealing now. They do say they do a blow job and a line of speed for a fiver, but I think a lot of towns have rumour like that.'

'I suppose you wouldn't want to find out.'

29

'No.' Seeing me laughing, he said, 'It is bad sometimes. Do you remember Martin Sowersby?' Martin had been Guy's friend at Sowthistle Junior School. 'He lived in a cottage at Ullestoft with his girlfriend, and he got on heroin. One night he told her he was off to walk their dog, and he went and hung himself in t' bottom of t' garden.

'They say Kirksfield police don't know what's hit them. There's a bloke supposed to be dealing out on Scottlesthorpe Road. He's bought himself this big house, like, and it backs on to t' river. You know you have to have fishing rights to catch trout in it? Well, Kirksfield coppers noticed there was always loads of cars parked outside his house, so they turned up one Sunday afternoon to raid him. He saw 'em pulling up and he recognized them and started chucking all his gear down t' toilet. He's supposed to have still been doing it when they came in.'

'On Scottlesthorpe Road? I can't believe it.'

'Neither could he, from what people say.' Guy sipped his beer. 'He certainly couldn't when they asked to see his fucking fishing licence. They thought he was having illegal fishing parties. When they couldn't see any rods and they saw there was no path from t' house to t' river, they fucked off back to Kirksfield. I keep telling my dad we should get some dope plants in t' sheds.'

We drank three more pints of Beck's, and at last orders we pushed out into the cold, where two policemen were watching people arguing, laughing, kissing and eating pizzas, and walked to Valhalla.

In the club red and green and yellow lights chased each other around the low bar and pool

30

tables. We stood at the bar and drank another pint, looking over at the dance floor, where a middle-aged man was tentatively touching the bottom of the woman he was dancing with. The DJ played Britney Spears, Jennifer Lopez and Steps, and every now and again a rap metal record that brought five kids with baggy trousers and long hair loping out of the snug and on to the floor.

'This DJ hates pop music, but they make him play it,' shouted Guy. 'He works at t' turkey factory but he says he's going pro.'

By half past twelve most people had either coupled off or settled down around their pints and bottles. The DJ put on 'I Am the Resurrection' by the Stone Roses and everyone on the dance floor walked off, while some single men in their thirties drifted on to it and played scraps of air guitar against their thighs. As the long instrumental part wore on the landlord walked over to the DJ, jabbed his index finger at the CD deck and at the men on the dance floor, and made an exasperated gesture. As the DJ looked for another CD, a broad-backed man with a broken nose and weather-reddened face came over to talk to Guy. I heard them mention the harvest, and pigs, and then I heard my brother say, 'We've got to sell up, like,' and for the first time I heard a slight reserve in his voice.

When we got out of the minicab at home, Guy went off to look at a sow that was pigging.

I stood in the yard with the pigs' snuffles and rustles in the warm sheds around me, and looked up at the bleary stars. When I heard Guy walking up behind me I snapped my head down. I was expecting him to say something sarcastic about looking at the sky, but he just stood next to me.

'What you looking at?' he said.

'Nothing in particular.'

'Are you looking at t' stars?'

'Mmnn.'

He looked up as well.

'I suppose it must be nice for you to see them. I always think it's weird in London when you can't see them for all t' lights.'

'Do you?'

'Yes, I do, as a matter of fact.'

'Oh. I wouldn't have thought you did.'

'I'm not saying it preys on my mind, like.'

'No, no.'

'No.'

And then he said, 'I always think it's amazing, like, you can't tell where owt actually ends. Like, if you were on a star as far away as we can see, you could see as far again in t' opposite direction. It just goes on without any end. You can't actually imagine that, can you?'

'I suppose not,' I said.

We stood not speaking for a moment, with just the sounds of the pigs rustling and a few lone cars passing along the main road.

'You're a bit philosophical tonight,' I said.

'Oh, you get very philosophical out ploughing on your own all day.'

'I suppose you do.'

'Come on, then,' he said. 'We've some more work for you tomorrow. I might even let you drive my tractor.'

On the Last Horse's Tail

The next day Guy and I mucked out more pigs, and began tidying up the haystack in the barn. After tea, my mum and dad gave me a lift back to York station. As we drove across the Wolds, darkness was gathering in the fields; from the car window I watched the lonely cream lights of tractors out late ploughing, and the black parliaments of rooks settling to roost in elms and sycamores beside the road. The birds kept changing places, flapping up out of the bare trees and circling above them, riding currents; ashy fragments floating on evening air.

I talked to my mum and dad about the sale, which would be in one month's time.

'Do you think you'll make enough to pay everything off?' I asked my dad.

'We don't know yet. Pigs and tackle's worth nowt, 'cause nobody wants little bits of stuff. But Bill Warburton reckons we should be all right if a builder buys t' yard for converting to houses.'

Bill Warburton was the local auctioneer and property agent whom my dad had asked to do the sale. It was strange to think that soon people would be living in the barn and the foldyard. 'Well, I'll come back and help you again next weekend, anyway.'

We fell into a comfortable car-silence as the dusk darkened and patterns of amber lights came on down in the Vale of York. On the radio, burbling low in the front, a newsreader said something about the winner of yesterday's St

Ledger race. The St Ledger is the Yorkshire classic horse race, held at Doncaster every year, and the last classic of the season. On St Ledger weekends when I lived at home, my mum always used to say, 'That's another summer over: they run t' St Ledger, and winter comes in on the last horse's tail.' She said it now in the car, although not the bit about summer being over. No one said anything.

I pressed my forehead back against the window, and looked out at more rooks restlessly rising and falling as if unable to find comfort anywhere in the landscape.

The Ballad of Pauline and Gordon

The Bensons had farmed smallholdings in Yorkshire for as long as anyone in the family knew of. Usually on these farms two or three men—the father and one or two of his sons—worked and drew livings from the business at any one time. When the sons married and had their own children, the new grandfathers snatched up their grandsons as soon as they could walk, and carried them along as they worked. The small children were wedged between tractor seats and gear levers as their grandfathers drove, sat in troughs while they emptied sacks of meal, and perched on straw-stacks as they built them up.

By the time they left school, these men were already strapped to a life, often bluff and ill at ease with the rest of the modern world, and prone to feeling unconfident in it. They passed on stories of their childhoods with fondness, but the world they

34

described sounded hard. If the men who worked on these farms loved the earth, it was only with the kind of love people had for the unforgiving Old Testament God who had cursed them with work, and who gave them their daily bread in the sweat of their faces, with no alternative.

My dad, Gordon, was an only son with three sisters. The family worked a small mixed farm in Marwood, a village in the Dearne Valley, which lies low in the Yorkshire coalfield to the west of Doncaster. The farm, with its sheds of dirty yellow stone and cold, damp house, was rented from the National Coal Board. The country was wild and industrial, the Bensons' land low and prone to flooding. All around, the views were crowded with collieries, farms, villages, factories, coal trucks and hills sloping up to the horizon.

Gordon's father, Richard, was a big, good-looking man, with a low, serious brow and curling dark hair. As a boy he had shown a talent for playing the piano, and a schoolteacher told his parents he should train as a pianist, but his father told him and his teacher they needed him for labour at home. As a man he worked six days of the week and did only the minimum on the sabbath. He loved Western films and grew flowers, and sometimes played the piano, but most of the time he kept his emotions hidden, and by modern standards his relationship with his wife Annie was workmanlike. His governing ambitions were to endure life, and to protect his family.

Gordon was big like his father, agile and bright working at home, but restless and unhappy at school. He disliked the teachers and the work at his secondary modern; his mind often fogged over

35

indoors and the teachers seemed to have little interest in their pupils anyway.

Before and after school he worked for his father. He rose at twenty to seven, fetched, fed and milked the cows, then went in to change his clothes and eat a breakfast of bacon and eggs. At twenty to eight he tied a full three-gallon milk churn to the handlebars of his bicycle, and wheeled it around the village hawking milk. When he had called at every house, he rode the bike home, and caught the bus to school. Arriving back at half past four, he got changed, ate a slice of bread and jam, and went back out to work again.

The only person he talked to about anything was Eileen, the oldest of his sisters and his friend. They shared a bedroom and she looked after him. They talked and talked, just about how they felt about things: people in the village, the farm horses, their loathing for the belly pork they had for tea every night, with its threads of meat among thick tallowy fat.

When Eileen was sixteen she began courting Howard Bullock from the village. Howard was a confident and impressive man who operated cranes and excavators on coal outcrops. He took Gordon to see the machines ripping away layers of rock, and Gordon thought Howard tremendous. When Eileen married him and moved to a house in the village, Gordon missed both of them.

At Bolton-upon-Dearne Secondary School he and the other farmers' sons bickered with the miners' sons about their families' industries. What was more important to the world beyond the coalfield: English food or English fuel? Who worked hardest? You didn't have to grow coal, it

36

was just there, you just dug it; aye, but farmers didn't work eight hours up to their neck in water, in the dark. They competed with details of death and injury: dads with their backs broken in roof falls and cousins with blue-black coal chips in their faces, uncles with skulls caved in by horses' kicks and brothers paralysed in falls from haystacks.

In the spring before they left school, boys who were going to work at the colliery were taken for a tour round it by men from the Coal Board. Gordon asked his form teacher if he could go with them, but the teacher said he knew that Gordon would want to work with his dad, and refused. In fact what Gordon wanted to do was become a butcher; he liked the idea of selling his food to people in a shop or from a stall, and he thought there would always be a good living in selling meat. But this was impossible, an idea lost in necessities like blood absorbed in sawdust, with just the memory remaining like a stain. Who would keep the farm going? His dad and mum were serious and practical, always working. You wouldn't bring up pipe-dream careers over the belly pork. You could help when your dad and grandad tied a pig to a post and stuck its throat, couldn't you? People always expected work off Gordon, but it did not feel as if they took him seriously. Aged fifteen he left school, and cleaved to the destined course of his life like a ploughshare cleaving cold soil in the autumn.

*   *   *

Seven years passed. Pits and farms thrived. In the Dearne Valley businessmen built new factories making nylon, glass, textiles and car parts. At Ash Farm, Gordon's father bought a tractor for the first time, and Gordon went ploughing allotments at half a shilling a go. Gordon bought denim jeans for working in, and a wireless so he could listen to music.

One day his younger sister Joan, now fifteen, brought a friend from school back to the farm. Pauline Hollingworth was a kind and pretty dark-haired girl, the middle one of three kids from a lively family. She loved animals in general and dogs in particular, and liked to talk. She was from Silverthorpe, a two-pit town that more or less joined with Marwood, and she differed from the dour Bensons. The Hollingworth men were miners, and she had a miner's ready, easy humour, but there was a levity beyond that. Her father, Harry, had been a pit shot-firer who, after an explosion left him with coal stuck in his arms and chest, gave up mining to drive lorries, delivering pop across the Pennines. He also worked as a singer and comedian in working-men's clubs. His nickname was Juggler, his speciality Widow Twankey routines; he could walk into any pub in the Yorkshire coalfield and be slapped on the back and acknowledged by name. At weekends he brought musicians, miners, comics and club people back from the clubs to his house for parties. Pauline's mum Winnie disliked this rowdiness, but Pauline liked it, or at least she did until everyone went home, and Harry and Winnie began arguing, and she put her hands over her ears and imagined the music back again.

The first time Pauline came to Bensons' farm for tea, she thought, 'Why are they so *serious*?'

They were quiet, and seemed cowed by work without an end. At the farm they had to switch Gordon's wireless off when his dad came in. At her house, the wireless was on all the time.

When she first saw Gordon come in from the yard and wash his hands in the sink, she thought he was handsome and tall, but diffident. At the table he said next to nothing, just murmured a few words to his father about a cow as he doused his meat in brown sauce. He was almost rude, but then she was quite relieved that his silence made him easy to deal with. She felt she wouldn't know quite how to act if he did talk to her.

In the summer, Joan asked her if she would like to come and stay for a week on the farm to help with harvest. Pauline came, and stayed in Joan's bedroom. It was a hot, dry summer, but she was distraught at how damp the house was, and then at the sound of the rats scuttling about in the walls, which kept her awake.

Gordon talked more when he was outside the house. Towards the end of the week, he began to tease her when they were working.

'Tha's leant yon sheaf up cock-eyed!' he would say, striding up to her and Joan as they stooked sheaves of corn in a sweltering just-cut field.

'Oh, not you!' she'd say. 'Bugger off!'

'Tha wants to watch thysen, or I'll get thee,' he'd say, falling to some stooking himself and stealing a look at her from the corner of his eye.

'Like to see you try!' she said.

She visited the farm almost every day as the heat of August built, and the work grew frantic. Every time Gordon saw her he would say to Joan, 'Eyup, I've to watch her, tha knows, she reckons she's going to thump me.' And Pauline would say, 'Oh I hate him, I'm going on strike if he's staying,' although if no one else was there, both of them privately felt self-conscious in their joke-hate routine.

One September evening after tea Gordon was in the farmhouse kitchen with Joan and Pauline. They had just cleared the table, and were putting away willow-pattern crockery, washing plates and sweeping the flagstones.

Joan unlatched the back door and stepped out into the yard to take some food scraps to the animals. Pauline wiped the tabletop.

'Tha's missed a bit,' said Gordon.

'You clean it, then.'

'I will if tha comes and mucks my cows out.'

'I thought I weren't any good at cleaning?'

'Aye, well.'

The kitchen fell quiet.

'I'm off to see what your Joan's doing.' Pauline walked towards the door.

Suddenly Gordon darted across to the doorway, and stood in front of her, blocking it with his hand on the latch. His heart felt as though it was going to burst in his chest.

'What are you doing, you daft a'porth?' said Pauline. 'Let me out.'

'Not unless tha gi'es me kiss.'

'You what?' Her eyes widened and she grinned in spite of herself.

'Tha 'eard,' said Gordon, wondering if he had really asked her to kiss him, or just imagined it.

She grinned, bounced up on to the balls of her feet and pecked him on his black stubbly cheek. Then she ducked down under his arm, and slipped out through the door.

From the yard he heard Joan's door-muffled voice ask, 'What've you been doing?'

'Me?' said Pauline. 'Nowt!'

*   *   *

The two of them began going to the Odeon in Silverthorpe to see Westerns, and they went for walks after Gordon had finished working, and watched hares in the fields. They went to the Doncaster Gaumont to see Norman Wisdom, where they laughed so much they cried, and they borrowed cars to drive out to the coast, past the power stations at Snaith and Drax, the animal-feed plant at Selby, and through the Yorkshire Wolds, with their remote farms, quarries and peaceful, bricky, pantiled villages.

Gordon's mum and dad were wary of Juggler, but Gordon didn't care. Knowing that Pauline liked him made him feel good, and strong in a way that he had not felt before. She took him seriously, and she absolved him of fear and worry. Pauline liked the way Gordon kissed her. His kisses felt how the kisses in the Westerns looked, when the hero in his buckskins took the heroine in his arms and planted his lips on hers. She liked how he called her 'sugar', and she liked how he warmed her feet between his hands.

Gordon felt that the trips out with Pauline on Saturdays, or the evenings when they were not working, were the clear, bright, free parts in his life.

*   *   *

41

Pauline's arts and humanities teachers put her at the top of her class in their reports, and when she left school at fifteen she used these reports to get a job as a kennel maid in Staffordshire. She agreed to start in September, but on the morning that she was supposed to leave the Dearne Valley, Juggler told her that she couldn't go, because her mum needed her help in the house. Pauline argued, and then ran upstairs and flung herself on to the bed, pressing her hot, teary face down into the pink candlewick bedspread.

Her mother sorted out a job for her at a haberdasher's in Burnsclough, a pit town two miles north of Silverthorpe. When Pauline told Gordon she was not going to Staffordshire, he said he was sorry, but he felt elated. He took her to see Cliff Richard at the Gaumont.

These were the middle years of the 1950s. Gordon Brylcreemed his hair, and bought a narrow-lapel black wool suit from a Doncaster tailor. He bought records by Little Richard, Adam Faith and Elvis Presley, and played them in the farmhouse on Saturdays when his dad was at Doncaster market and Pauline came round, and they made bacon and cheese sandwiches together. Their favourite was Little Richard's 'Tutti-Frutti', and they sang together the refrain that went 'Awopbopaloobopawopbamboom!' When Pauline wasn't there, he sang it to himself, and when he went out to feed the cows, he sang it to them.

Pauline befriended some girls who came to the shop to buy dress material, and went with them to dances in the working-men's clubs and hotels, and sometimes up at the Mecca Ballroom in

Wakefield. She didn't ask Gordon to go: dances didn't seem like his sort of thing, and she was enjoying herself enough as it was.

Now when he asked her to go out she um'd and ah'd, and that made him afraid again, so he stopped asking. She came to the farm less and less, and eventually they didn't see each other at all any more. One of Gordon's friends started going to pubs and dances, and got Gordon to come along as well. Girls asked him to dance because he was tall and handsome, and he began to enjoy it. He took some of the girls out, and he thought about Pauline only when they misunderstood something he said or did not get one of his jokes.

Or when conversations petered out.

Or when something went wrong with him and his dad, and he had no one to talk to about it.

Or sometimes in the day, when he looked across the field towards Silverthorpe.

*　　　*　　　*

One evening in June, just after tea, Gordon was sitting in his work clothes reading the *Yorkshire Post* when there was a knock at the farmhouse door. His mum answered, and came back into the kitchen to tell him he had a visitor. As he passed her, she whispered that she thought it was a policeman.

Gordon recognized the man, a miner known to people locally as Sun. Sun was Pauline's uncle.

'Eyup, lad,' said Sun. 'Does tha know who I am?'

'Aye, I know thee. What's up?'

'I want a word wi' thee.'

43

They stepped away from the house. Lowering his voice, Sun told Gordon that Pauline had sent him a letter, but had had no reply.

Gordon was puzzled. He had received no letter. 'It must 'a got lost . . .' he said.

'Never mind what happened to t' letter.'

Sun said that Pauline had written to Gordon because she had had a bit of trouble; one morning as she was waiting for the bus to take her to work, a man at the bus stop had touched her legs. When she got on to the bus, he sat near her and stared at her all the way to Burnsclough. She had been frightened. Her mum had reported it to the police, and there had been a court case at which the man pleaded guilty. Pauline wanted to tell someone about it.

'She says tha's t' only person she could talk to, lad.'

Gordon walked to Pauline's with Sun without going back into the farmhouse.

They fell into conversation easily. He felt as if he had relaxed for the first time in months, and she thought he was better looking than she remembered.

They both felt like best friends. He warmed her feet between his hands.

*   *   *

And then they were courting properly. They watched Westerns and went to the coast and, more than anything else, they walked. Miles and miles through the lanes between the fields, watching the animals and looking at the wild flowers and talking and talking and talking. Their friends made

44

innuendoes about their walks, which annoyed Pauline. 'We *were* looking at blinkin' rabbits!' she said. 'That's why we waited till it were dark!' Their friends also asked why they didn't come to the pub instead of always traipsing about the fields, and so one night they went to the Crown in Marwood, where Eileen worked behind the bar. They sat at a copper-topped table with a pint of Barnsley bitter and a Babycham, and suddenly they couldn't think of a single thing to say to one another.

'Shall we go?' asked Pauline as Gordon drained his pint.

'Up to you, sugar,' he replied.

'Come on, then.'

As soon as they walked out of the door they fell back into conversation. This was very strange, they agreed, but, well, that was just them.

They had been courting for two years when Pauline went on a week's holiday with three friends to the Butlin's in Pwllheli. The day she got back, Gordon heard a rumour that she had been off for a moonlight swim alone with another man. He felt angry: he had thought he would never hang on to her, and here was the proof.

'There were a great big group of us, you gormless bugger,' she said when he questioned her about it that evening. 'We'd all been to a dance. If you don't believe me you can hump!'

'Well if that's it, you can bugger off!'

'I bloody well will bugger off!'

She slammed the door on her way out.

He knew he had been wrong, and the conviction did not fade even after the harvest and Christmas had passed. He made excuses to himself to drive up past the shop where she worked, and began going to get his hair cut in the barber's next door. One day, almost a year after their argument, he met her in the street as she was sweeping out the shop. After an awkward conversation, he asked her if he could take her out that Sunday night. She told him to meet her outside the fish and chip shop in Silverthorpe High Street at half past seven.

He knew this was his last chance, and that night he felt nervous as he washed off the scent of the cows, and Brylcreemed his hair. He borrowed his dad's car, and called to pick up his friend Dickie Durdy. As he waited outside Dickie's house, he noticed he was tight for time. Maybe he should have told his dad he had to come in sooner. Bloody hell . . .

It was twenty to eight when he got to the fish and chip shop, and she wasn't there.

Standing on Silverthorpe High Street on a warm spring evening, Gordon Benson faced the defining moment of his life. He looked past Dickie and down the High Street where other people, groups of lads, groups of lasses, were having fun, shouting to one another, the life of the town moving easily past and through them. Morris 1000s, Ford Anglias and Austin Healeys rolled by. Girls wobbled by on stilettos; boys in slim black suits and white shirts lent their arms, with hands scrubbed red and fingernails chipped, to steady them. Somewhere down the street a girl laughed.

Gordon clenched his own scrubbed hands, and took a deep breath. 'Come on, Dickie lad,' he said.

He got in the car and drove to her house. Her mum said that Pauline had gone to a dance at the Pavilion Club in Wath-on-Dearne, five miles away. He jumped back in the car, floored the accelerator all the way, and as he pulled up outside the hall he told Dickie to go in to check that she was there.

Dickie came out and said yes, she was inside. They went to the pub across the road to wait until the dance was over. A few men and women, sweating, hair peeling out of Brylcreemed sweeps and beehives, came in; Gordon looked at each one anxiously, and tried to keep an eye on the club through the pub window. When he saw the crowd begin pouring out, all bright, sweaty and steaming in the night, he got up and walked over, but she spotted him first, and slipped past without him seeing.

He waited until the last groups had wandered off, and then suddenly he and Dickie were standing alone in the light, sweet wrappers and cigarette packets on the floor, and an old man in a flat cap waiting to lock up.

'Drop me off at her house and then take t' car home will tha Dickie?' said Gordon. 'I'll walk back.'

She was still up, sitting in the back room with her dad. He had made her an Ovaltine and fired up a Player's, and they were listening to Fats Waller on the radio. When Gordon came in, she froze.

'Now then,' he said.

Juggler stubbed out the Player's, and stood up from his chair. 'I'll be off to bed,' he said, and left the room.

'Will tha marry me, Pauline?' he said. *'Please?'*

'Oh, go on, then,' she said. 'Warm my feet and I'll think about it.'

An Accident

They married two years later, on a wet Easter Monday in 1963. They moved into a two-bedroom house on a lane leading down from the farm, and Gordon began taking a weekly wage out of the business for the first time in his life, ignoring his father's claim that this would lead them to bankruptcy. In the winter he worked nights bulldozing snow from the roads with the tractor so that cars and coal lorries could get through for the early morning shifts at the pits. Pauline got a new job at the grocer's in the village, and she soon knew everybody; when housewives came in to ask if the bread was fresh, she learned from the grocer to say, 'Better than fresh, love, it's tomorrer's.'

Pauline painted the kitchen cupboard doors in different pastel shades, the way she had seen it done in a story about American kitchens in a women's magazine. They bought a Staffordshire Bull Terrier puppy. In the front garden she planted deep-red roses.

Three years later she gave birth to me. My grandfather carried me about the farm in his arms. His hands were very big, twelve inches from thumb-heel to little-finger tip, and when we walked across the fields in the evenings, my hand felt the size of a postage stamp in his hard, square fist. When he took me out with him on his red Nuffield 465 tractor, which like all tractors in those days had no cab, I perched on the broad round mudguard, holding on to the head-sized rear spotlight, with his bear arm curled around me to

48

stop me falling backwards.

My grandmother Annie, a soft, black-haired woman with flowery pinnies and large smiles, died of throat cancer shortly after I was born. After her death my grandfather barely spoke for six months, and spent his spare time cutting down trees and chopping them into logs and sticks, until he made piles six feet high. He told Pauline that when Annie was alive she had always been asking him to chop more firewood for her lest she run out, and he had always put it off, though he knew it would anger her. Gordon watched him from the kitchen window.

One day in August my grandfather was rolling pea silage in the yard while my dad greased and repaired the Massey Ferguson combine harvester. He was getting it ready because that morning they had waded through the barley fields and bit into the ashy-gold grain and decided it would be ready to cut the next week.

At six they went down to Gordon and Pauline's house where Pauline, six months pregnant with their second child, had put ham, cheese, bread and apples out ready for them.

The roses were in bloom and my grandfather joked about stealing some of them. As they were setting off back to the farm Pauline, putting the dishes in the sink, saw Richard nip a flower off between his sausagey index finger and thumb and twirl it at her with a smile. She wagged her finger in mock annoyance. He winked, put the red rose in the buttonhole of his smock and walked up the lane to the yard with his son in the golden dust of harvest summer.

They began again, working through the last of

the warm, dusty daylight. As Richard rolled the silage heap, Gordon was tightening bolts on the combine. Suddenly he heard a loud, deep, iron crump across the yard. He let the guard fall on to the cogs and ran. The tractor was upside down on the ground below the high end of the silage clamp. It was upside down and his dad was underneath it, flung to one side with the mudguard across him. The spotlight was embedded in his chest. Gordon shouted to him, and then felt a wave of shock. The next thing he knew, Ossie Blower, the pit ambulanceman who lived opposite, was there telling him to sit down.

'Is he dead, Ossie?'

Ossie closed his eyes and made one slow nod. Gordon just wanted to get the tractor off his dad's body, but the men who kept coming through the gate and into the yard told him to stand back and take it easy. They would do it: they were bringing a breakdown truck from the garage in the village. Gordon said a breakdown truck wouldn't work. They thought he was losing his mind, but when they tried to winch the tractor up, the front end of the truck rose into the air because the tractor was too heavy. They brought all the car jacks from the garage, but they sank beneath the weight of the tractor because the ground was soft with juice from the silage.

Back down the lane Pauline was still washing the dishes in the kitchen, with front and back doors open to let the cooling evening air blow through. She heard the fast, fast fall of running feet, and then a neighbour, Pete Fisher, who worked on the railways, was in front of the window! Shouting: 'One of 'em's under t' tractor,

50

Pauline! It's tipped over and one of 'em's underneath, love.'

But which one?

She froze, with her hands in the sink. Unbreathing, she felt spasms and pain in her chest. She tried to run out of the kitchen, but she couldn't move her legs, and they felt like lead, as if they were paralysed. But then somehow she was in the lane with the world swimming about her and someone, she didn't know him, running towards her. He held her back and breathed into her face, 'It's all right love, it's all right, it's not Gordon, it's his dad. Gordon's trying to get him out.' He was physically restraining her now. 'You don't want to go up there, love—'

Up at the farm Gordon got on another tractor, reversed it, put its rear hydraulic arms through the holes in the Nuffield's rear wheel, and lifted them. That moved the tractor clear, and he saw his dad lying on the ground, red rose petals scattered across his chest and shoulder. An ambulance came, and after they loaded Richard inside Gordon climbed into the back. Looking out of the rear window he saw Eileen jump out of Howard's car, and run towards him, and then she was climbing in with him. The ambulance rattled out of the yard, and took them to Doncaster Infirmary.

On the way Gordon figured that his dad must have got to the top of the silage and slipped the gear stick into second rather than reverse, by accident.

In the Darkness

The sun kept shining, and out in the fields the barley ripened, its dry, thin, whiskery heads bending over against the stalks like the skulls bent against the crooked necks of the old men who leant on the field gates, talking about the accident. In the yard, and at home, Gordon did not discuss it. While his sisters settled funeral arrangements, he worked, greasing machines and sweeping out sheds.

At two o'clock on a hot afternoon in August, the pall-bearers lowered Richard Benson into the dark clay of Marwood churchyard, beneath the church tower, stone barns and colliery headgear. Gordon Benson walked away from the church in which he had been christened and married, and knew then that he would never by choice go back to the grave.

Two days later he climbed up into the seat of the combine harvester, twisted the ignition key and coaxed its engine, pulleys and sprockets into juddering life. Noise and urgency pushed aside care. He eased up the clutch pedal and headed out of the yard towards the fields.

It was a good summer. The nights were hot and malty, the dews holding off so that the grain stayed dry until two o'clock in the morning. Gordon harvested into the night, and when his neighbour who was carting the corn went home, he stayed alone, taking the trailer loads of grain back to the yard himself. On the third evening, at some point after Ronnie had cycled off home, he lost his sense of time: all his thinking was there in the yellow, mothy headlamp beams, the straight swathes, the rabbits bolting out of the barley in his path. It might have been midnight or two o'clock, or four o'clock for that matter. He had become unaware of the time just as he was unaware of the dust in his nose, or his booted feet playing the hammers of clutch and brake or his hands vibrating to numbness on the chipped Bakelite steering wheel.

Something settled on his right arm. A warm leathery pad, like a big hand. He jerked, startled: and then he heard his dad's voice saying, 'Tha's done enough for tonight, lad. Come home.' Gordon pulled up, lifted the bed of the combine right in the middle of the row, and drove it back to the yard as fast as it would go.

On the winter evenings when he snowploughed with a hessian sack hooded over him against the cold, Pauline would sit up with him afterwards until the icicles and chilblains faded out of his face. Now, in the warmth of an August night, she sat up with him looking into a face all brown and burned from the sun, and she listened to him as he told her what had happened in the field. He laid his head in his hands on the kitchen table and sobbed, and the tears left pink lines on his dusty face. When they closed the curtains of their bedroom, there was light coming over the fields.

*   *   *

Three months later, Pauline gave birth to their second son, Jonathon, at home. He had a defective heart, and although the doctor said he would live through it, he died at six weeks. It was early one evening when Gordon was at work. Jonathon

53

began a crying that Pauline could not soothe. She called the doctor, who told her not to worry: young mums always worried and thought everything was a life or death matter. She tried to be calm, but when she could no longer pretend that the crying was not, in fact, a squeal, nor that his face was not turning bluish, she telephoned again and pleaded, weeping, while next door's husband went up to the farm to fetch Gordon. The doctor came, and Pauline saw the truth on his face as soon as he looked at Jonathon. He called the hospital. Gordon came running in, and when he looked at the doctor, the doctor looked away from him.

Gordon and Pauline buried their second child in the same grave as Gordon's mother and father.

The next thing was the farm tenancy. On rented farms sons usually took over tenancies when their fathers died, but the National Coal Board had a new land agent with plans to consolidate holdings. The agent refused to pass on the tenancy, making no apology and expressing no regret.

This was enough. Together, with Pauline pregnant again, they began looking for a new farm to rent outside the Dearne Valley. They looked in the Wolds villages they used to drive through on the way to the coast, and after a year's searching they found Rose Farm, named after John Rose, who had built it in the 1840s, and who had claimed to be a spirit medium and faith healer. The farmyard opened on to two lanes, the one running past the churchyard and the other leading away past houses into fields on either side of a low valley. Four of the fields, including one with a spinney of beech, larch, plum and elder, belonged to the farm—sixty acres altogether, small as farms

54

generally went, and one of the smallest in the village. Gordon thought he could make it pay if he worked for other farmers and rented fields roundabout, and borrowed money from the bank to buy it at auction.

At the start of the summer Pauline gave birth to a baby girl, and they named her Helen. A few months later, she and Gordon piled me, Helen, the farm cat, two dogs, assorted tools and a kettle into an old Vauxhall saloon, and drove us up into the hills to start again.

The Settlers

They dug up the roses from the garden in Marwood and replanted them in the new garden. They put bullocks and milk cows in the foldyard, and built sties and farrowing pens in the old stables and sheds. They put lambs in the garden, and hens in the hen loft, making nesting boxes from orange crates provided by the man at the fruit shop in Kirksfield who bought their potatoes. In the four fields my dad grew wheat, barley, hay and potatoes in rotation. He sold the potatoes to merchants, and to fruit and fish and chip shops in Kirksfield, feeding those that were rotten or too small to the pigs. The wheat went for animal feed and biscuit-making, and he sold half the barley for feed and kept the rest back for his own stock.

After a year at Rose Farm, my mum gave birth to another son, whom they called Guy. When she was helping my dad in the fields or in the yard she carried Helen and Guy along with her in cots and prams, standing them on the soil, cobbles or among potatoes in a trailer. When I came from school I tagged along with her or my dad.

They made friends: Myrtle, a beaming Billy Bremner of a woman who loved the church and was captain of the ladies' darts team, and her husband Arthur who drove trucks at the gravel quarry; Joan, the Methodist daughter of the village joiner, who knew everyone, and her husband Ken who sometimes came to help with the potatoes and told jokes to me, Helen and Guy. The youngest of Myrtle's sons, Karl, came to work at the farm when he left school, and then in summer while he and my mum looked after the yard my dad went contracting, cutting corn for other farmers in the area. In the summer mornings we used to drive out with him to the farms he was working at, and then leave him there to drive the combine. In the late evening Mum put us on to the back seat of the car wrapped in blankets and drove to pick him up, and we imagined ourselves to be like cowboy-settlers heading to the frontier in covered wagons.

They bought more breeding stock, raising the total to more than 100 sows and five boars, and bred pigs that they sold to bigger farms for fattening. Some with weak abdominal walls became ruptured and therefore less attractive to buyers; some of these my dad had killed at a local slaughterhouse, bringing them home to butcher on the kitchen table. Usually he suspended the carcasses from hooks in the scullery ceiling until he had time to chop them into joints. This could lead to embarrassment for Helen, Guy and I when friends came to visit and caught a glimpse of four long, white, lifeless half-pigs swinging upside down

56

next door to the living room.

'What's that hanging up in that room?' they asked.

'Pigs,' we said.

'Pigs?!'

'They're dead, though.'

'Dead?!'

'Let's go outside for a bit.'

We measured out the weeks in joints of pork: hams, legs, loins, sausages, fried bacon, boiled bacon, gammon steak, pork chops, liver with mushrooms, ribs with sage, roast shoulders with apple sauce, chips fried in oil rendered down from leaf fat ripped off the belly, trotters for Juggler when he called on his way to the coast, brawn for Auntie Eileen and Uncle Howard, hearts cooked up for the dog. Every three months I came home from school with Helen and Guy to find a butchering in place with the kitchen stinking of the protein rankness of fresh meat. On these afternoons we filled in the hours between school and tea by couriering bags of pork around Sowthistle to Mum and Dad's friends. These gifts of joints, chops and trotters, allocated according to the known taste of the recipient, would be repaid informally with apple pies, chrysanthemums, cabbages and carrier bags of damsons left on the stone doorstep, although this was no compensation for those who had to deliver them when they would rather be watching telly, or playing football with the other kids on the playing field.

The pigs we bred were good, and began to fetch top prices. The contracting was working. European money was coming into agriculture, and down on Kirksfield Airfield the wartime bomber

57

hangars were converted to storage for EC grain. In one of the four fields we pulled up a hedgerow to make the field bigger and burned it on Bonfire Night with Joan, Ken and their kids, roasting potatoes in the ashes. We went on holidays to Devon before the harvest, and my dad traded his old car in for a brick-red Volvo estate, chosen on the grounds that it had sufficient room for carrying a ton of potatoes down to the fruit shop in Kirksfield.

It was going better than my mum and dad had dared to hope for when they bought the farm at the start of the 1970s. In fact, looking back at Rose Farm as the 1980s rolled around, there was only one thing that was not quite right. Me.

Family Values

'All tha's to do is keep it straight, and watch to see nowt gets caught up in t' tines,' my dad said as he stood on the step of our big green John Deere 2140 giving me instructions, and I sat in the driver's seat trying to look confident. 'And don't look so worried, lad, there's nowt much can go wrong. Tha tries too hard, tha knows.'

It was a cool autumn half-term evening, and I was about to try hard to power harrow one of my dad's fields. The power harrow was a machine about the size of a double bed that was pulled by a tractor through ploughed soil to produce a finer tilth. Although it could get jammed and damaged if you were unlucky enough to fetch up a buried piece of old abandoned machinery, it presented no

58

challenges to most people capable of driving tractors, and was a typical job to give to a boy in his mid teens, like me. I felt good being trusted with it, and encouraged by my dad telling me that I worried too much. I eased up the clutch and set off up the edge of our field. With the machine rattling and banging behind me, I even felt a sort of cockiness.

However, after about ten seconds, I noticed the tractor bonnet pointing away from the hedge despite my attempts to rein it back with the steering wheel. After fifteen I became aware that I was going backwards, and after eighteen I heard a terrible wrenching over the top of the engine. I disengaged the power, and looked back and around to see what had happened. It was bad. Somehow I had caught up the hedgerow in the tines, and roughly ten yards of hawthorn bush, roots and all, had been pulled into the machine until it stuck fast. I got off the tractor and walked around the mess scratching my head as if I knew what I was doing, just in case anyone was watching. Then I got back in, turned off the engine, and went looking for my dad.

The power-harrowing accident confirmed what had long been suspected by everyone at Rose Farm, i.e. that my tendency to get things wrong was not really down to youth or inexperience or bad luck, but to a near-total lack of concentration, coordination and instinct. When it came to farm jobs, I was generally useless, a liability, a danger to the people, animals and buildings around me. I couldn't steer straight, couldn't keep my mind focused, couldn't even shoo a pig along without falling over or letting it run through my legs. Mal

59

and Karl looked nervously at each other when I climbed behind the wheel of a tractor. My dad tried to gee me up, but that just made me feel guilty. Boys on some farms got beaten for ineptitude like mine.

Operating machinery was one of the hardest jobs for me, because it required you to do half a dozen things at once when I found it hard to do one. However, what I disliked even more than that was repairing machinery. Every bit of our tackle seemed to be full of bolts that would shear and belts that would snap within an hour of starting to use it, this typically happening after waiting several weeks for conditions to be dry enough. Everyone would crawl over and poke inside the machines enthusiastically offering ideas, while I tried to join in and trapped my fingers. When there was no solution to be found, we would stand waiting for the repairman from Warkup's agricultural engineers to come bouncing into the field in a red Ford Escort van, and I would wonder how on earth some people got pleasure from this sort of thing. I envied people like that, and I particularly envied the Warkup's repairmen. With their oily overalls, white smiles and giant steel boxes full of parts and tools, they seemed more at ease, both calmer and chattier, than us. Our life must have looked quite idyllic to people on the other side of the hedge, and my dad was making a good living, but we always had to worry about something: machines breaking, animals dying, or too much or too little rain. I wished I could be an engineer.

*   *   *

60

'I should think they are bloody happy,' Dad said one sweltering afternoon as we stood in a field beside a broken-down baler, waiting for Warkup's.

I was sixteen, and with sixteen-year-old tactlessness had just pointed out that the world of the Warkup engineers seemed more cheerful than ours.

'They'll be on overtime every night from July to September, and they start charging when their van leaves t' yard. I don't charge from when we leave Sowthistle to come here.'

'No.'

He lifted the guard of the baler, and started cleaning out the dust and bits of barley awns. The field was owned by Smith and Crosby, businessmen from Hull who were investing in land, which with the new European subsidy payments for grain now offered a safe return on investment. Their manager wanted the baling doing quickly so he could get his ploughing done.

'Come on, give us a hand with this.'

I poked about in the dust and got it in my eyes. This made me feel annoyed by what I considered to be my dad's fatalism in the face of issues such as happiness and broken balers.

'Why don't you, then?'

He looked up, surprised white eyes blinking in the black, dusty face. 'Why don't I what?'

'Why don't you charge 'em from when you leave Sowthistle?'

He straightened up and removed and then refitted his cap. He had an expression of almost weary bewilderment which was becoming familiar.

'Because when we go contracting, we charge by t' acre, don't we? We don't get paid for just

61

standing about.'

'Oh, yeah.'

There was mild astonishment in his voice at my forgetting this basic fact, which was fair enough. Plenty of kids my age were out with balers themselves, and some just a couple of years older were doing their own contracting. So the blunt patience felt, in the tense, adverse circumstances, almost like a reproach. I assumed that he was struggling to tolerate me, and that he probably hated me for not knowing how to operate the baler. Thinking about that made me resent the situation myself. It was all right saying we did not get paid for just standing about, but then we were *not* just standing about. We were leaning at angles to push our arms deep inside a large machine to remove accumulations of dust-and-grease goo. Some of my friends from school had jobs in shops.

We worked on without talking, my dad concentrating on trying to fix the chain or whatever it was, and me brushing dust from the wheels and sprockets. I decided to rescue things by being matey like an engineer. I waited until enough time had gone by to show that I had understood how we charged by the acre not the hour, and then called over to where he was working, 'Did you enjoy it in the Sixties, Dad?' I had been reading *Shout!*, Philip Norman's biography of the Beatles, and enjoying all the stories about pop music and swinging London.

'Eh?' he said, from somewhere inside the machine.

'Did you and Mum enjoy it in the 1960s?'

He slid out from the cogs and belts, which suggested he thought my question was more

62

serious than it really was. 'Enjoy what?'

'All the music and that. The Beatles and . . . all that.'

He gave up trying to work out the link between the broken baler and his life in the 1960s. 'It didn't really affect me and thy mam,' he said. 'You heard about it, but most people's lives were normal.'

'Oh,' I said.

'Have you got that wheel clean?'

'Nearly,' I lied, and I began working furiously, yanking the wheel around.

'You're knocking that dust on to me now, look. Go steady.'

'Sorry, Dad.'

*　　　*　　　*

My dad was patient, and tried to get me to rely on my instincts: 'Tha tries too hard'; 'Don't look so worried'. Mal told me not to fret and said, 'When all else fails, try brute force and ignorance'—but I didn't have any brute force. Karl said, 'Just *do* it and don't think about it'—but what comes first, believing you can do something, or being able to do it?

I couldn't just do those things, and it was hard to explain the admiration and jealousy I had for those who could. Once at teatime my dad said that he had been talking to the headmaster of Sowthistle School, and the headmaster had described someone as being 'an educated type—not like you, Gordon, practical'. My dad said he felt as if the headmaster might be patronizing him, and I got angry and said that of course he wouldn't have been. I told my dad that he didn't know what it was like not being able to do things, and then felt bad because it probably made him feel worse.

Guy, meanwhile, was emerging as a sort of child prodigy. By the age of ten he had assembled his own rudimentary toolbox and was making useful things out of wood. By eleven he was reversing trailers with a one-handed nonchalance. By twelve he was growing vegetables in a patch of the garden behind the barn, having constructed an elaborate netting system to keep hungry birds off his seeds. He didn't talk about it—he just came home from school, changed his clothes, and ambled out to thin out a row of onions or pull up some weeds. Even before he graduated to proper crops and tools at the age of about fourteen, he had come to regard school as an inconvenience to be got out of the way each day before getting back to the vegetables or tools.

Occasionally, briefly, something would capture his interest and pull him up to a teacher's excited attention. While showing no interest whatsoever in the sport, he had a talent for rugby and played for the school team before giving up; despite an indifference to art, when invited to draw a mother-in-law's tongue plant he became interested in its leaves and drew an intricately detailed picture for which the teacher awarded him an A, and then showed no further interest in the subject for the rest of his school career. It seemed to me that as he walked off into the world of animals and vegetables, the universe beyond slowly melted away.

The chief objects of his affection were cats. There were usually between fifteen and twenty living around the farm, sleeping near the boiler in the outhouse, but a new stray turned up when Guy was twelve, and they befriended each other. When Top Cat died, he took others, which followed him about and seemed to stand apart from the other cats. He picked them up and rubbed them against the side of his face and smiled. He said he respected the cats because they did not tie themselves to him. He liked how they came and went, and did not demand affection when he did not want to give it.

It wasn't long before Guy could be relied on to do most things better than me, and so I settled for the idiot jobs: torch-shiner while they worked on mending fences; gate-opener when they were moving pigs; maggot-scraper when they cleaned pens out; flint-picker in the fields while they ploughed and harrowed.

I had more in common with Helen, who although she liked the pigs, seemed to live on a different plane altogether. She was an abstracted little girl, happiest playing alone in a small wooden hut in the garden, climbing on straw-stacks, and swinging in an old tyre suspended from a beam in the barn. Her favourite things were animals and fairy tales, and she said frequently that she wished she had been born a dog. When she and I worked on the farm, it usually involved us being directed by Guy.

My dad must have wondered what was happening. He worked hard and the farm was doing well, but while on other farms the children were looking after the animals while their parents took holidays, or going to discussion groups and bringing home new ideas, I was becoming a village joke, Guy was bizarrely self-absorbed and Helen was becoming a vegetarian. 'One day we're stroking them and giving them names, and the next thing you know you're taking it in a bag to someone or eating it!' she complained regularly, after the point in her early teens when she connected the meat to the pigs down the yard. She tolerated chicken, beef and lamb for a few years more because she thought all meat other than pork was a delicacy, but by the time she was sixteen she had converted entirely to fish and vegetables. 'You wouldn't have dared not eat meat when there was rationing,' said my dad.

'No, but there isn't rationing any more,' said Helen. 'Far from it when it comes to pork in our house.'

*   *   *

When I began to get good marks at Kirksfield School, people came to regard my relationship with my family and the farm as a source of amusement. My mum told visiting relatives that if she could combine Guy's hands with my brain, she would have the perfect son. Old Albert Wheatley, a pensioner who sometimes watched us as we worked, worried about my dad.

'Got you cleaning that baler then?' he said, walking past one day in the summer holiday and noticing that I had been entrusted with removing loose barley straw from the machine.

'Oh, aye,' I said back, trying to copy his warm, resigned tone.

'Aye,' he said. 'I suppose you'd come on a lot better if it told you how to do it in a fucking book. I don't know what your father must fucking think.'

66

'Well, no,' I said. 'I don't know either.'

Looking out of my bedroom window over to the weathervane that night, I thought about writing my dad and mum a letter of apology, but couldn't think what I'd say. I wished I could find an obscure skill to redeem myself, and then I wondered if I could do something with the pigs. I liked working with them—I was just scared of doing something wrong when someone else was there. I tried to think of a small job I could do that might make people say, 'Oh, he's no good wi' t' machinery but he's grand wi' t' animals.'

The only thing I could come up with was looking after ill pigs in my school holidays. Sometimes they got ill and were put into pens on their own, and thinking that I might be able to help them, I began trying to nurse the sick pigs back to health. It was easy but time-consuming, i.e. ideal for me, and in some cases just helping them eat and drink would bring them back round. Sometimes I made a hay-bale pen for them in the barn and went to feed, water and bed them up while Guy and my dad and Karl did something more important.

No one ever did say, 'He's grand wi' t' animals', but the possibility always seemed to be there, and I thought I had got a chance for glory one spring when a sow in the midst of giving birth got a piglet trapped across her cervix. Dislodging the piglet in such cases is not difficult: all you have to do is get your arm inside, push your first two fingers into the cervix, and pull the piglet around so its head is pointing towards you. You just have to be comfortable with inserting your bare forearm into a sow's birth canal, and to have a hand which is not

67

so wide at the knuckle that it makes the sow uncomfortable. My dad sent me to bring a bucket with warm water and soap. As the swollen sow lay moaning on the floor, and Karl and I watched, he rolled up the shirt sleeve over his right arm, soaped up, and tried, but his fingers would barely go in. Karl tried and got knuckle-deep, but the sow began twitching. I thought my time had come. I can't say I was excited about the idea of putting my arm in there, but I felt that a calm, manful approach would only enhance the shift in the way everyone regarded me. I rubbed soap on, kneeled down at a right angle to the sow's bottom, and under the four expectant eyes, inserted thumb and finger tips into the bright pink distended labia. My fingers seemed to be going in fine, but I felt a sort of tight tube of muscle squeezing them, and she groaned. My damned hands! They obviously looked less masculine than Karl's, but were still too wide because, as the relatives had informed me, I had inherited them from my grandad.

'Ah, well. Go and ask thy mam to call t' vet,' said my dad. 'See if he can come straight away.'

I must have looked quite upset because when I walked past Karl he told me not to get down over such a daft thing. This, however, made me feel even worse. I had my own reasons for not wanting to look stupid in front of Karl.

Karl

Karl, seven years older than me with a mind as quick as rabbits and muscles like potatoes crammed in a sack, embodied all the confidence and abilities that I wanted, but did not know how to get. For Karl, strength and agility were like crafts in themselves. He lifted four-stone potato sacks up above his head on one flat palm, and leapt clean over five-bar gates, just to show himself that he could. He ran along the very edge of haystacks to feel the rush of knowing he could fall but wouldn't, while I implored him not to because it made me nervous.

He seemed happy and well equipped for the world, and I wanted to be like him, or at least to be his friend. If he and my dad had an argument about something on the farm, I got embarrassed because I thought he would hold it against me. I asked him to teach me how to copy some of his feats of strength or machinery operation, but unfortunately, since he liked boxing and martial arts the most, he concentrated on them, and spent most of the time showing me how to punch hay bales. Sometimes when we were bedding the bullocks up, him cutting the bales and me holding the twine, he would turn and sharply jab the air near my jaw.

'What did you do that for?' I asked, the first time he did it.

'To teach you to always cover yourself,' he said. 'Never leave y'sen open.'

Karl's reputation spread beyond Sowthistle.

69

After studying boxing, he became Valhalla's most feared bouncer, and spent Saturday nights taking fights apart single-handed. One evening when I was about thirteen, I met him on the main street in Kirksfield. He was with a girl and dressed up for a party, and I suddenly saw that his flamboyance went far beyond holding bags of potatoes above his head. With his open-necked black silk shirt, cowboy boots, flapping flared trousers and cowboy moustache, he looked like a Mediterranean nightclub millionaire who had been sent to size up the town for its potential. He looked at my Adidas sweatshirt and jeans, laughed, and said, 'What the fuck you wearing? You'll never pull t' birds dressed like that, you chump.'

'Don't care about lasses,' I mumbled. I was slightly dazed by Karl's tip, because it made me realize for the first time that men and women went out at the weekend with the sole intention of finding someone to have sex with. Just what I needed: something new to worry about.

Women and animals, he charmed them all. Sometimes when I'd finished my jobs I would go looking for him, and find him on his hands and knees in a pen, face to face with an intrigued bullock that he had befriended. 'Watch this,' he'd say, seeing me come into the pen, and then he would head-butt the bullock. The bullock butted him back, and then Karl butted him again. After a few minutes of this he grew bored and, chuckling to himself, walked out of the pen. 'It's barmy, that beast,' he said.

Local women were captivated to the point of hypnosis. I noticed that girls passing the farm gate blushed and smiled as soon as they sensed his presence in the yard. Even the older, married women were susceptible, a fact which had its practical uses on a farm located in a village. One morning a young woman called Mrs Sykes came running into the yard from the back door. She was new in the village, with one child at school and another at the playgroup, and she looked shaken. My dad and Karl were penning sows up in the foldyard. 'Can you come, Mr Benson?' she said. 'There's a pig!'

They rushed out of the yard, Karl vaulting a five-bar gate with a foot to spare, and my dad running along after him. Mrs Sykes ran along after my dad, arms folded. 'We'd've brought it back but we're frightened it'll bite!' she said.

'A sow'll not bite you, love,' said my dad. Pigs escaped all the time, and he was feeling confident of a routine recovery operation—but then he noticed that just ahead of him Karl had stopped at the corner of the school, and was looking down towards the village hall, and then back at my dad with a pained expression, resting the finger of his left hand against his forehead. My dad heard the high-pitched shouts just before he reached the corner himself, then looked down the hill to see the last bit of the pig's rear disappear through the open double doors of the village hall. There were screams. Women poured out of the hall and stood on the grass in front, clutching the hands of small children. The pig had entered the village hall on the day of the Sowthistle toddlers' playgroup.

My dad and Karl stood behind the school wall like two soldiers who had found themselves behind enemy lines and spotted a heavily armed sentry post. 'Tha'll have to do it, lad,' said my dad.

71

'No way,' said Karl, but they both knew the truth. If women were involved, there was only one solution.

It was as if they sensed him coming before he arrived, striding into their midst in tight T-shirt, flapping flared jeans and boots. Even the angry mothers relaxed when he told them the pig wouldn't bite them if they were quiet. He stepped into the hall, leaving an expectant throng on the grass waiting for bangs and crashes, but instead there was only silence. After thirty seconds a snout sniffed the air at the door and the long, rolling, bristly mass of pig emerged into daylight with Karl behind it, urging it on with masterful slaps to its waggling hams. As he brought the sow back to Rose Farm, the women called out to thank him and he raised a hand to acknowledge them without turning his head.

Karl's sexual prowess seemed to me to have a physical incarnation in his metallic-red Ford Capri, which he kept parked beside a straw-stack at the bottom of the yard. On the boot-lid rim, next to 'Capri', he had added in gold adhesive letters the name 'Koff', given to him as a child by his dad because of his asthma. On Sundays he and my dad would drive the car on to two planks over the grain pit and work on the underneath, shining torches, and discussing possibilities and theories about its engine and gearbox. On summer Saturday nights I watched him roar out of Sowthistle and head to the coast, to charm young women on holiday from the West Riding. Some Sundays, girls turned up in the afternoon and rode with him on the tractor for half an hour, and I stayed away from him, shy of his confidence.

Once he let me sit in the Capri's passenger seat, and drove me round the village. I sank back into an interior that was fetid with seduction. There were dice and leopardskin-print covers on the bucket seats, and the dash, which sat level with my eyes because the springs in the passenger seat had gone, was covered in short-pile black fur. The gear knob was a glittering piece of cut glass, and around the edge of the ceiling, edging the side and rear windows, was the sort of gold fringing you saw on the bottom of expensive sofas. In a box near the handbrake were cassettes, all either classical or country and western—Tchaikovsky, Rachmaninov, Don Gibson, Dolly Parton. Karl hated pop music. He said it had no feeling, although he did like the Howard Jones video for 'Like to Get to Know You Well', in which Howard walked around a city centre shaking hands with strangers. Karl said that would be his greatest ambition, just to go up to people and talk to everyone. I thought he wasn't doing a bad job as it was, especially with the female population of the East Riding.

'Fucking hell, Karl!' I said as he steered out of the stackyard and up towards the pond at eighty miles an hour.

'Passion wagon, lad,' he said.

'Can you see wi' all that fringing?'

'Birds love it, man.'

'Is that why you put it in? For birds?'

He gave me a look, and as the pub and the post office passed by in a blur, I tried to act as if I knew what he meant. Privately, I was worrying that I would never even pass my driving test, let alone have sex with a girl in a car. For Karl, who seemed to move through life, and let life move through him, with ease, it all seemed as simple as drinking water from a stream: he just cupped his hands and held them there while he took what he wanted.

Not being like that, and fearing that he would see me for the uncoordinated bag of nerves that I really was, I made jokes at my own expense to make him laugh. When I tried to spear a rat with the hay-fork and missed, I told him a funny story about misthrowing a cricket ball in games. When he asked me to bring him a tool, I brought the wrong one on purpose. They were not very funny jokes, but they made him laugh, and we seemed to get along OK.

I would have been happy enough spending all my spare time carrying stuff around for him and getting rides in his car, but of course I couldn't. I was getting older, and someone else was about to throw a rope around my imagination and pull.

The Kirksfield Madonna

My good marks at Kirksfield School led some of the teachers to contrast my enthusiasm with Guy's apparent indifference. One afternoon as we stood in the kitchen after school, Guy told me that Mr Leonard the history teacher had asked him why he couldn't be more like me. 'Oh,' I said, with a plunging feeling. 'What did you say?'

Guy seemed surprised that I asked; he did not seem bothered, or indeed interested, by Mr Leonard's observation. 'I just told him I wasn't you,' he shrugged, and went out to look at his vegetables.

74

I sat with a smart, wise-cracking boy called Stuart Hopkinson, whose dad farmed in a village near Highthorpe. Stuart's mother had died when Stuart was young, and two aunts had stepped in to bring up him and his two brothers. He never spoke about his mother and, in an observance of decorum rare among teenage boys, no one ever asked about her. He did not talk about his dad's farm much either, and most of the time we talked about pop music.

We went to see bands: Adam and the Ants at Hull City Hall, ABC at Scarborough's Futurist Theatre, and Madness at the Bridlington Spa Hall, where we were chased by bikers who were hanging around trying to ambush mods. Sometimes we went with other kids who liked music, and we became good friends with a boy called Billy Hodgson. Billy was himself a biker, but he had a love of pop that had led him, at the age of thirteen, to present to our English class a talk about Abba so passionate that the teacher herself allowed it to overrun as the class rained questions upon him.

When we were sixteen, Billy and I stayed on at school while Stuart left. He ended up working at home. Most boys whose fathers had trades left at that age, and many of those who had anything to do with farms couldn't get away fast enough. We saw each other out in Kirksfield every so often, when we would revive school jokes, and exaggerate the escape from the bikers in Bridlington. Slowly we became acquaintances waving to each other on nights out at Christmas, across bars that weren't really too crowded to push through.

I sometimes thought that I would have liked to have been drawn back into the bosom of the family business myself, but as it was, in the sixth form I found myself being drawn to a bosom of a very different kind.

Mrs Hirst, my English teacher, wore expensive clothes, courted controversy, and was married to a successful architect. Sometimes she wore leather trousers. She gaily denounced other teachers in her lessons, and told us that she, rather than the biology department, ought to be teaching sex education, because who the hell didn't know that the meaning of sex was emotional rather than scientific? Mrs Hirst told us about Noam Chomsky's theory of universal grammar, and said that Freddie Truman's criticism of the Yorkshire cricket establishment made him a modern folk hero. When she taught us *The Mill on the Floss*, she slapped the table in front of us and said Maggie Tulliver's persecution was typical of small towns. We knew she was talking in code about herself and Kirksfield, and she made us feel as if we were on her side, as if we should be trying to get away.

The two escapes she seemed to propose were simply leaving town, and poetry. Mrs Hirst approached poetry like a sort of religion. When she taught us the poems of Seamus Heaney and Thomas Hardy, she said poets lived higher lives than ordinary people, and that living these lives allowed them to reveal the truth of human experience in instructional form. This was what a poem was: a set of beautifully written instructions dealing with aspects of day-to-day life such as love, ignorance or pleasure. Seamus Heaney's *Death of a Naturalist*, for example, was a coded instruction to disbelieve whatever adults had told us about sex. Thomas Hardy's 'The Immanent Will' was meant to warn us about vain, pompous adults such as one might find, for example, in the Kirksfield School staffroom.

Of course, to understand these instructions you needed Mrs Hirst's guidance, and in delivering it she became to the boys and girls who fell for her the very Madonna of Kirksfield, the leather-trousered medium by which the Truth might be manifested to her pupils.

We couldn't work her out. Did she mean it, or was she just showing off? Why didn't she write poems herself? Was it right to say everyone was stupid if you were cleverer than them? Was Mrs Hirst a visionary, or just a snob?

I could see her faults, but that did not stop me having cups of coffee with her when she invited me into her office. She often asked pupils in after lessons, usually on their own, to talk about their work. She wanted to get to know people, she said, because then she could help them get the most from the books. She asked about our personal lives, and I had never felt as indulged and sophisticated as I did the first time I sat in Mrs Hirst's office, and she invited me to discuss myself and my family. It was like being a poet. Her office smelled of Benson and Hedges cigarettes, which she lit and waved about airily, and of coffee, which she made with an avocado-green Braun filter-coffee machine. She shook in the ground coffee loosely from a jar instead of spooning it, and drank her strong brews black with two sugars, holding the cup in the same hand, with its red fingernails and Celtic rings, as her cigarette. At home I stopped drinking tea, and found in the back of the cupboard with my dad's shotgun, a boxed filter-coffee machine which had been a Christmas present from a relative some years earlier. I put it in my bedroom and bought filter coffee and drank it black. 'You want to watch yourself with that coffee, you'll make yourself poorly,' said my mum, proving conclusively how misunderstood people like Mrs Hirst and I were.

Once Mrs Hirst asked me about my dad, and I recklessly told her about not being able to do mechanical things. After that, sometimes when we studied Seamus Heaney's early poems about his estrangement from his father, she shot me knowing looks over her book. I was embarrassed by this; I didn't even like Seamus Heaney's early poems, because I did not think they contained any answers to the problem of conflict with your parents. The later poems like 'The Flax Dam' and 'Lough Neagh Sequence' were all right, but I wanted to know how he had sorted out the conflict with his dad, and he never got around to that.

*   *   *

Mrs Hirst said I should go to university to study English. I said I'd like to go to London because I couldn't think of anywhere else, and because there seemed to be a lot of things to do there. Mrs Hirst said that was a good idea, and got the forms and helped me to fill them in. When it came to the 'interests' bit, I said I didn't have that many, and she asked me about things that I had done. I said I spent a lot of time with my dad and, flicking the ash off the end of her cigarette, she said, 'Let's put farming down then.'

'No,' I said, but then somehow ended up telling

78

her about how I got put in charge of the sick pigs in the summer holidays.

'Right,' she said. 'Put "the prevention of pig disease", then.'

'Pig disease?' I said. 'Are you sure?'

'Yes!' she said. 'It'll make you stand out. They'll think you a very interesting candidate.'

'I should think it fucking will,' said Mal when I told him about it that teatime, riding on the step of his new tractor up to the fields to bring some straw down. 'Does tha think she can get me into college, then?'

Mal thought that I was making life hard for myself by going to university, but as he also thought life was meant to be hard, this made a sort of common ground between us.

'Don't ask me, Mal,' I said.

'Is that what they teach thee, looking after poorly owd pigs?'

'Not as far as I know.'

'What is it tha's doin'?'

'English.'

'English what?'

'It's just studying books,' I said, and tried to change the subject to the bull that Mal had recently had the fight with, but he was interested in Mrs Hirst. 'What is it she's wanting tha to learn?'

'It's hard to explain, I just think she thinks, like—oh, I don't fucking know.'

And I fucking didn't.

But I was offered places, and on results day Mrs Hirst, dressed in a sheer black jersey dress, with faint coffee-fag odour on her breath, hugged me, and then stood back, holding me with her hands on

79

the knobs of my shoulders, and said, 'You see! It was all worth it!'

*   *   *

I went to London University to study English Language and Literature. On the day I left, my dad got rained off from combining so he came home at lunchtime and drove the whole family to York station. They waved me off on the platform, and as I watched them slipping away I thought they looked sadder than I had expected them to. I bit my lip, and kept thinking about them all the way to London.

Farmer's Hands

Five weeks after I arrived in London, my mum and dad came to stay with me for a weekend. It was the first time they had been to London since their honeymoon. They said it was just a visit to see how I was settling in, but on the Saturday morning, after we had eaten cornflakes and my dad had shaved, and I thought we were leaving to go and look at the Houses of Parliament, they sat down and said they needed to tell me something. There was an outstanding feed bill. Something about a feed company amalgamating with another one, and the new management wanting all the money paid within a few weeks. The point was, they would have to sell the pigs to raise some money. They had talked to Karl, and he had got a new job on a pig unit out somewhere near York. Now that

Helen, Guy and I were grown up, my mum could spend more time in the yard.

'Don't you worry, though,' said my mum. Then it went quiet, and she said, 'It's getting to be a very small world, and I don't understand it. We went to Scarborough one night and saw a boat in the harbour from Belgium with four hundred tons of potatoes all for McCain's.'

When I arrived back home for a visit in November, Mum and Dad were both out picking potatoes, and Helen and Guy were at school. I walked around the yard on my own. The sties were all empty and the gates and the chains linking them clanged, amplified by the vacant sheds.

*   *   *

They started over again, though. In the summer holidays I used to take three weeks off at the start and then go home, working with them on sunny days, doing essays when it rained, and reading the coursework books late at night while minding the grain pit to make sure the auger carrying the grain up to the bins did not jam.

As the time passed, Guy left school to work at home and do a day-release course at agricultural college. Helen went to university and then worked as an assistant at Sowthistle School, coming home after her second day to announce that teaching children was 'like watching little lights come on', and that she was going to train as an infant teacher.

I liked being in London. I liked how you could find people to talk to about anything, and how all the districts were so different from each other.

The only problem was that there seemed too much of it all for it to feel like a home, and although I visited dozens of areas imagining that one day I would walk out of a tube station and think, ah— *here's* the place that *I* was meant to live!—I never did. In Bloomsbury there were not enough parks; in Finsbury Park, too many wide roads; in quiet Muswell Hill, too many old people. In the end, I settled in one of the quieter bits of Finsbury Park, because it was friendly. People from all over the world move there to make new homes for themselves, and people who are trying to make new homes tend to be generous to others doing the same, although it took me several years to work that out.

It also took me years to learn that most people feel that they don't quite fit in from time to time. When I found the other students at university intimidating, I assumed that I was in the wrong place with the wrong people. Ignoring the fact that plenty of other farm kids from Yorkshire had been to university and enjoyed themselves, I decided that in my case, the experience would just have to be suffered and endured. I thought of Sowthistle as the place I really belonged to, and without realizing it, I re-adopted the two survival tactics that I had learned there.

The first was to try to keep people happy or, even better, amused, in order to distract them from whatever they might think was wrong with me. One of the easiest ways to keep people happy is by appearing to be what they would like you to be: being cack-handed with tools and pigs had been fine when I made myself out to be a sort of village idiot with O-levels. The problem with this

82

tactic was that if you arrive in London with a northern accent, a thick neck and a background in pig farming, what many people expect you to be is a blunt, down-to-earth, practical person. This is why I spent many years pretending to be someone whom I knew very well I was not.

I am ashamed to think of how ridiculous this was. Some people on my course nicknamed me Beefy, and I let them. I let flatmates think that any small repair I did around the flat indicated considerable DIY ability. I allowed a girlfriend to take my fat, square hands in hers, stroke them and say, 'Farmer's hands', even though they were *not* farmer's hands because they were so soft and pink that every Christmas Guy, sitting next to me at the tea table, laid one of his toughened, broad paws next to mine and said, 'Office hands'. The first time I brought a friend home, a cockney girl called Alison who was studying French and wanted to see the countryside, she said, 'I can't *believe* how all your mates think you're so bumblin'.'

We had been out with my friends in Kirksfield the night before.

'I did try to tell you that,' I said. I had, but no one had taken any notice.

'Funny, innit?' she said to my mum. 'In London everybody thinks he's like *Last of the Summer Wine* or summink!'

The second tactic was to work all the time. I don't know if I had picked up the farmer's idea that nothing is ever finished, or if my own experience of farm work had made me think that if something wasn't hard, I couldn't be doing it right. But for one or other of these reasons, and because I liked the work, I spent most of my spare time writing essays that ran to ridiculous lengths, and trying to read everything on the reading lists even though it was obvious no one was expecting me to.

Of course, you don't have to be a neurotic Yorkshire farm kid to use work to muffle the hums of self-doubt and worry. If you have a long essay to finish, or a large field to plough, or a house to clean, or a car to mend, you can tell yourself that you don't have enough time to wonder if it is really a good idea to try to keep everyone happy without asking what would make you happy yourself. You end up thinking you're too busy and that you will do anything for a quiet life, and you notice that you seem to be your calmest in the moments when you are alone. This approach to life helps you get a lot of work done, but it is not exactly beneficial to your relationships.

The summer I did my finals I met a girl from the course called Jo. She was a left-wing intellectual with long chestnut hair, who lived in a flat owned by the Labour Party and had friends in countries like Mexico and Czechoslovakia. She was the sort of girl I had thought I might meet in London, and at first I was so awestruck that I took her advances as a joke: when she told me, after our nineteenth-century literature tutorial, that she liked my smell, I thought that either I must have BO, or that complimenting people on their smell was something left-wing bohemians must do. She told me later that she had meant my deodorant.

It was only as a result of getting drunk at an end-of-term party that I got up the nerve to go outside for a walk with her and end up snogging in the garden. The next morning, lying on a mattress in a flat in Finsbury Park, Jo stroked my fingers

84

and became the second person to say the thing about farmer's hands.

'Shush,' I said.

'Ooh, shush!' she said, mimicking my accent. 'Are you sorting t' woman out?'

'I just don't have farmer's hands,' I said. 'Tell me about your mate in Mexico again.'

Jo found out our finals results the night before everyone else (it turned out she was two-timing me with our Marxist nineteenth-century literature tutor), and met me in the pub on Trafalgar Square with a bottle of champagne and told me I'd got a first. We drank the champagne and then I asked her if she could wait for me a minute while I went over to Charing Cross station and called home from a payphone. My dad answered the phone.

'I've just got my exam results,' I said.

'Oh have you? Did tha pass?'

'Yes. I got a first.'

'I should think tha did.'

An announcement over the loudspeakers echoed around the station. I wondered if he meant, 'I should think you did because you'd have been wasting time for three years if you'd done anything less'? Or 'I should think you did because I think you are clever and you deserve it'? I can't remember what we talked about during the rest of the conversation.

The same night, Jo suggested that we go to a work camp in Czechoslovakia. In August.

'What do you mean, you have to go home?' she said.

I told her why.

'Are you mad? You're an adult!'

I told her it was hard to explain, and then

85

called home.

'Will you be able to manage if I don't come, Dad?' I said. 'I might be able to come later.'

'Aye, OK, lad,' he said breezily. 'We'll be all right. Get off and enjoy yourself.'

I realized with a jolt that they did not, in fact, need me at all. 'Oh, right,' I said. 'I will.'

In the end, Jo and I lost interest in each other well before August anyway. I lied about having applied for a visa for Czechoslovakia, and then told her that it hadn't come so that I didn't have to go.

But I did stay in London, in Alison's flat in Pimlico. I worked at a hotel reception desk and as an office cleaner, and I enjoyed it. At the end of that summer, despite what was or was not in my own head, I really belonged to the city far more than I did to Sowthistle or to Rose Farm.

*   *   *

I had planned to study for a PhD after college, and become an academic, but one day towards the end of the last term, I stood in the department corridor and thought about the tutors behind the office doors. It dawned on me—I know I should have thought it before—that being an academic was going to involve a lot of time in 1960s office buildings, talking to people like them. Most of the men seemed full of suppressed anger and were having affairs with their female students, and most of the women seemed to get their fun from playing complicated word games. I tried to think of something else that involved writing and reading, but that would give me a more lively, varied relationship with other people, and thus came with rather idealistic expectations to journalism.

I wrote for a few magazines and newspaper features desks, and applied the same rules to journalism as I had to university—work hard, give people what they expect, enjoy yourself in the pub. I got a job as a section editor at the magazine company where I was working when my dad called to tell me about the sale. I didn't go home so often any more, and I got promoted, and felt as if I had a solid career.

I didn't feel particularly relaxed with most of the people I met while working, although this seems to be common to many journalists. To be fair, it is not hard to find people who will confirm your sense of yourself as an outsider if you work in the profession in London. It did not help my self-esteem when an editor told me, one day when he realized I did not know the name of the river that flowed through Oxford, that he had given me the job because he had confused me with another Richard who had been to St John's College, nor when a woman from the East Midlands, who seemed to be trying to make friends with me, told me that I would never be one of the in-crowd in London journalism because I was 'fat, northern and working class'. ('I'm not even working class,' I tried to explain to her. 'Technically, my dad's a capitalist.' 'Well, that's what people *think*,' she said.)

I didn't talk about any of this to anyone, of course. I just wished I could apply the approach that I imagined Karl or Guy or Mal would have done. 'Just get on with it! Tell them all to fuck off!'

I thought less often about how I should never

have left Sowthistle, but when I got a mobile phone in the 1990s and I was walking along a city street feeling low, I sometimes invented a reason to call my brother at work, because talking to him when he was out in a field driving a tractor, or messing with a pig in the yard, made me happy. That is, the idea made me happy. The conversation itself was usually brief.

'Hello Guy,' I'd say, walking down Upper Street.

'Now then, what's up?'

'What you doing?'

'Power-harrowing at Jim's. Why?'

'I just wondered.'

'Are you all right?'

'Yes. Um, the gears on my car have gone a bit sort of grindy . . . do you know what it might be?'

'Sounds like t' linkage's worn.'

'What've I to do?'

'If you're comin' up I'll 'ave a look for you, but best to take it to a garage.'

'Right.'

'I shall have to go cos I'm comin to t' end of t' field.'

When I clicked the phone off I felt numb and made myself think about something else.

*   *   *

I got promoted, I moved to a pleasant flat, and I travelled abroad. When I went home to Yorkshire, these things gave me a feeling of security, and I felt all the lucky novelty of being paid for work that came easily. I realized that doing it made me as happy and confident as Guy was among his

88

vegetables. I moved along a chain of relationships with loving girls who started off believing that I was sympathetic and kind with a sort of earthy edge, moved through a period of incomprehending resentment during which they would ask me why I didn't talk about us, and finally agreed that we should break up. I recommenced the relationship with Jo, who had left the tutor, but this ended after a month with a depressing argument. I remember that she kept asking me what would make me happy, and I kept saying that I didn't know, but then I didn't think anyone really knew what made anyone happy. She said I must know some people who *were* happy, and I said I would try to think of some. To my surprise, the first person who came into my head was my brother.

History

If, as a historian, you were to look closely at a particular village in a particular part of the Wolds at the end of the 1980s, you could see Guy Benson working with Gordon and Pauline Benson, with a new herd of pigs, the four fields, and the contracting. You could see them blaming themselves when a volatility in the new globally-interconnected economy set off a swing in interest rates that set off uneasiness in a Kirksfield bank manager that led to him offering them the commiserating advice, as endorsed by the Ministry of Agriculture, Fisheries and Food, that in the modern world a farmer really had to specialize in one area if he or she were to keep up with the new science and technology. You could see him suggesting that because of this, the sale of the four fields in order to clear the overdraft was probably a blessing in disguise. You could see Jim Croskill buy the fields, all but for a small spinney of larch, birch, pine and elder hedge which sheltered a pig shed, and thus you could see Rose Farm, once home to pigs, lambs, hens, cows and bullocks, become a specialist pig farm.

And then you could see them trying again with more pigs as Helen Benson left to go to university in Liverpool, and Guy began working the four fields for Jim Croskill, and he and Gordon and Pauline worked their weekends, gave up holidays and tried to control the overdraft secured against the value of the yard. You could see it getting more difficult to turn a profit, and you would be able to find certain mistakes, oversights and problems that were particular to Rose Farm. You could see the Bensons alternately optimistic and pessimistic as the prices swung, and if you were to pull away and look at the other farms in Sowthistle you could see this was partly because those farms were, with the new crop and livestock science, producing more crops and animals which led to gluts on the market.

And if you were to pull back a little further, you could see the new Tesco in Kirksfield getting busier, and the food on its shelves acquiring the immediate, entertaining, novelty values of pop music. Near the market square you could see the grocer's where Gordon used to sell potatoes closing down, and other small shops also closing, and the small producers who supplied them with ad hoc half-dozens and half-tons looking instead for whatever contracts they could find with the Winterswick bacon factory. And at the Winterswick bacon factory you could see managers telling their would-be suppliers that the trouble was that they now needed to buy from big producers because that's how you got a consistent product, and people wanted consistent products at a cheap price, even though at that moment in another supermarket you could also see a woman saying to a man at the butcher's counter, 'Well, I'm a person and I don't want it', and the man laughing at her.

And if you were to pull away until you saw the whole of England you could see the producers of certain crops and stock receiving subsidy cheques that rose in value with the farm output; cheques which accelerated the process of the big getting bigger and locked the country into a global muddle born out of the panicky fear of hunger at the end of the Second World War. You could see many farms selling off their machinery to clear overdrafts, and putting all the land out to contractors who competed to farm it at the lowest prices, and many others being swallowed up into vast farmed estates of tens of thousands of acres. And you could see the cheques administered by a desk-bound bureaucracy and accompanied by manilla envelopes fat with forms. Most, though not all, of the talk on those farms concerned efficiency, which is to say making more for less; after all, this is what the subsidy system set out to encourage, and it was the mantra of the processing plants and supermarkets who, as they reminded producers when their costs rose, were now at liberty to bring in cheap food from Poland or Holland or the Far

East far more quickly than they had been able to in the past, thanks to all the new roads being built in Europe and cheap shipping across the globe.

If you were to pull back further to see all of Europe you might find at the end of those roads bold new headquarters of chemical companies which employed deskfuls of economists to monitor subsidy payments and adjust pricing in accordance with any change in them, and laboratoryfuls of people working on genetic modifications which would allow their employers to patent seeds themselves. And if, finally, you were to pull away to see Earth looped with those blacktop roads and shipping lanes and air arcs, you could see moving along them the great surpluses of food, bought cheaply on one continent by one of the great global commodity dealers and then sold at a profit on another, bending and bowing the economic rules by which the local producers played.

Move back, and rest above England. If you listen carefully, you can hear a few, a very few people, suggesting that the rush to gain cheaper food is leading to the loss of something which might be officially out of date but somehow seems a good thing that it seems wrong to lose. The British mixed farm was a creation of the enclosures in the eighteenth and nineteenth centuries and had by the end of the 1990s all but disappeared. Its point was to combine livestock and arable so that a) if one crop failed you had others as back-up, and b) there was an interlinking of production in that you could feed crops to the animals, and fertilize the land with animal manure. To many people unfamiliar with agriculture, this seems so perfect and commonsensical an idea that

92

they are vaguely surprised to find out that it is now an eccentricity, a defiance, a tourist-centred enterprise. For some of the few people who murmured about something good being lost, this is one of the cases of money defying common sense that encapsulates that jarring, perplexing fact of the modern world: that the logic and geography of business is not syncopated with the logic of human feelings.

If now you close back in on England eight years after Gordon and Pauline and Guy sold the four fields, five years before Gordon will walk with me around his old barn that has been converted into a fashionable house, you will see Gordon on the telephone to me one Sunday night in summer. Pig prices have been going down, and of course this time there is nothing else to sell but the yard.

'I think it'll go back like it were in t' Thirties,' Dad says, and I worry, but then wonder if he might be worrying too much. Farmers are always predicting that things will get as bad as they were in the Thirties, when farming was so unprofitable that land stood derelict.

A month or so later, in a brief telephone conversation with Guy, he says something about the farm being done for, and I'm not sure how seriously to take him.

A few months after that, one morning as I am getting ready to go to work, Dad calls again and says, 'Um, Richard. Me and thy mam's got a bit of bad news for thee.'

Tractors

I went up to Sowthistle again the weekend after I had been home to help with the first preparations for the sale. On Saturday Guy and I began dragging stuff out of the sheds so that we could sort it into saleable and non-saleable piles. Lots of the tools were old and broken, but Guy dropped them all in the selling pile with the newer stuff.

'Bill Warburton says to put owt like this in,' he said, after I pointed out that the wire baskets had holes in them. 'People buy it for their gardens, or hang it in pubs.'

It was strange to think about the things we had used being put in gardens. 'That seems sad to me,' I said, and Guy laughed. 'Doesn't it bother you?'

'I think using tools to decorate your garden is extremely sad, but I can't say it bothers me personally.'

'I just meant—'

'I know what you meant. But I'm not bothered. I just find it slightly bizarre.'

'Maybe Bill could *advertise it* to antiques dealers!' I said brightly. 'Or people who do film sets?'

He stopped brushing cobwebs from a steel milk churn, and rolled his eyes. 'Half of t' people at t' sale'll be fucking antique dealers, you twat! They all watch out for t' adverts for farm sales in t' *Yorkshire Post*. I'm hoping we get somebody who wants a Ford 6610 for their patio.'

The curvaceous blue-and-white Ford 6610 was the tractor Guy used. 'Maybe one day somebody

94

will,' I said.

'No reason why they shouldn't,' he said. 'It's a beautiful tractor.'

After we had sorted everything that we could move ourselves, Guy went to fetch the Ford to move the larger implements that were left. I walked across the yard and idly rubbed mud from another tractor, a thirty-year-old Leyland 255 with a muck filler on the front. Most of the farmers in Sowthistle had an old machine like this somewhere, a model from the 1960s or 1970s that was either still in use, or left to sleep in a shed like a rusting four-wheeled pet. In some cases this was down to thrift, but in others it was linked to something more powerful: a straightforward but unspoken affection for agricultural tractors.

When Guy and I were growing up, most young boys in Sowthistle knew the model numbers of Fords, Internationals, Massey Fergusons and John Deeres, and spent afternoons racing them down green lanes on their bikes. Guy could quote the horsepower and torque of popular models by the time he was six. I liked the logos best, but we both loved the look of them: the blue-and-silver British Leylands, the outlandishly shaped new red Massey Ferguson 595, and the impossible square size of mustard-coloured Muir Hills. On car journeys we kept tallies of the different makes we saw in fields. At the annual Kirksfield Show we picked up posters and leaflets showing tractors photographed in sunflare and casting powerful shadows over fields, and Blu-tacked them up on our bedroom walls. In Guy's bedroom, we organized model tractors on a toy farm and allocated them jobs.

At senior school we realized that the wider

world regarded tractors far less favourably. Boys from Kirksfield thought they were amusing machines that somehow entranced yokels, while English teachers introduced us to tragic vignettes in which machines destroyed natural landscapes and perverted the human senses. *The Grapes of Wrath* and 'Cynddylan on a Tractor' depicted the loud, snub-nosed machines that we loved not as exciting wonders of the modern world, but as monstrosities creating a rift between nature and humanity. Of course, few authors and teachers had suffered from deformed ankles, as men who ploughed with horses had, but we didn't know about that. Most of us just fell for the idea that life was more natural, and therefore better, in the tractorless past. Aged about thirteen, inspired by his own stories about Suffolk punches and Clydesdales, I informed my dad that I would have liked farming more if it had still been done using horses. 'Tha wouldn't say that if tha'd to get up at five o'clock in winter to harness them up,' he said, teaching me in five seconds everything that anyone ever needs to know about nostalgia.

While I lost much of my interest in tractors at Kirksfield School, Guy joined the small cult of boys whose passion had intensified in the face of criticism. At the time, this passion was being vigorously stoked by *Power Farming*, a radical new magazine which applied the values of *Loaded* to farm machinery. Unlike the earnest and erudite *Farmer's Weekly*, with its long features and pages of market digests, *Power Farming* celebrated the exhilarating capabilities of new technology—the pleasure of tearing up a muddy field with 250 horsepower at your disposal. It was full of large colour photographs, and the journalists wrote about new agricultural machines in the way that motoring journalists write about sports cars. Implements were not simply efficient or well made but, as you heard groups of boys sitting in the library reading out to each other, 'awesomely powered' and 'acre-gobbling'.

Power Farming belonged to a new approach to agriculture which was like a rural version of the 1980s yuppie greed-is-good philosophy, and which made kids like Guy feel part of a new generation rebelling against old-time stick-in-the-muds who held things back. As the 1980s wore on, older farmers complained about *Power Farming*-loving lads from the agricultural colleges wanting to spray everything, even the undergrowth in hedge bottoms. To them, Guy said to me once, the new technology was like taking away the skills they had learned about controlling weeds through winter. It made it all too easy. Sensing their frustration, some lads would affect a ruthless and reckless approach to wind them up even more.

The line separating tractor fans and everyone else was usually clear, although it could be crossed. David Arnott, whose dad owned a small farm on the vale to the east of Kirksfield, remained in the *Power Farming* set until he was fifteen, but then took a sudden interest in the pop group Japan, and began dressing like their lead singer David Sylvian, in pointed suede boots and full facial make-up. He avoided questions about the transformation by being enigmatically silent.

More surprising than this, however, was the crossing in the other direction. Mike Skelfe joined our school in the third year when his family had moved out of a well-to-do suburb of Hull. He was good-looking and a punk, with bondage trousers and Sex Pistols T-shirts: girls fancied him, and boys admired him because he swore at teachers and would sometimes just walk off the pitch in games to go and smoke a cigarette.

The change in him began when he started working weekends at a pig farm in his village. He remained as the lead singer of the punk group he had formed for some time, but after a few months he switched sides in a sudden defection which I was there to witness. It took place during a football match in games, on a dreary day in the autumn. Mike drifted away from the game and stood on the touchline, looking out over fields beyond the fence. Mr Bradshaw, the teacher refereeing, was an old-school disciplinarian who disliked Mike, and seemed to take this personally. He stopped and stared at Mike, and gradually we all stopped, and stared at him.

'*Mike Skelfe!*'

Mike ignored Mr Bradshaw's bellowing, and peered harder across the fields.

'*Skelfe!*'

Peer.

We knew Mike had heard him. We awaited the punk reply.

Mr Bradshaw, reddening, stalked across the pitch to him and yanked him back by the shoulder.

'What the hell do you think you're doing, lad?'

Mike pretended to notice him for the first time, and said, 'I'm watching yon tractor ploughing.'

Mr Bradshaw looked like a man who felt someone speaking a foreign language might be insulting him. He briefly looked at us, as if we

98

might be part of some practical joke.

'What do you mean, watching a tractor?'

'I'm watching it ploughing! That Massey yonder, look. He's making a real good job on it.'

Bradshaw gaped at him, and we gaped at Bradshaw, and that was the end of Mike Skelfe the punk.

After this, Mike drifted away from the people he used to hang around with. They laughed at him but he seemed to enjoy it, perhaps seeing this as another act of rebellion. His interest in ploughing became famous around school, and soon everyone claimed to have seen him looking over hedges at the Massey ploughing. The boys in the band said it was put on, but had to reconsider when after leaving school at sixteen he took the job on the pig farm permanently.

*   *   *

Guy roared into the yard on the Ford and reversed it into the shed. 'Let's move that,' he said, indicating a forty-year-old wooden turnip drill which would have excited the antiques dealers more than the ex-*Power Farming* readers. 'You can drive t' tractor if you want, and I'll put it on t' hydraulics.'

'No thanks,' I said. 'I think it's best to match people's skills up to the right thing.'

'That depends if t' right thing's available.'

'Well, yes.'

He climbed into the tractor cab and grinned down at me out of the rear window. 'Do you remember your power-harrowing incident? That bloody hedge—'

99

He was about to re-tell a story that is always guaranteed to make him laugh, but was interrupted by the voice of our sister calling our names in the yard.

'Uh-oh,' he said.

Helen

My sister Helen teaches infants at a primary school in Hull. Her colleagues say she has a natural gift for education, and small children find her strangely attractive, but she is not a stereotypical schoolteacher. For one thing, her main interests are pop music, shoes and football. For another, she has a talent for catching escaped pigs. And for another she has an unusually robust way of expressing her opinions. As a teenager she once punched a boy in the face for saying that she had no right to criticize Liverpool Football Club.

For these reasons, she is one of the few people I know who intimidates my brother.

She put the tin tray of coffee mugs down on the ground, looked at us, and then at the littered contraptions. She pointed at the turnip drill. 'What the hell is *that*?'

'A turnip drill,' said Guy defensively.

She raised her eyebrows, and walked around the drill looking at it as if something might emerge from its dusty tubes and hoppers to explain its existence. 'You don't grow turnips, though.'

'Dad used to,' said Guy.

'We *used* to use slates in school. Rather recklessly, the County Council felt it was safe to

100

get rid of them once the computers were installed.'

Guy looked as if he was doing a piece of long division in his head, and kicked mud off the tractor's front wheel.

'Maybe Dad wanted to keep it for sort of sentimental reasons,' I said. 'Or he thought it'd come in useful.'

'Of course,' she replied. 'A handy little turnip drill! Always a comfort.'

Guy and I blew on our coffees.

'I got chatted up in Valhalla last night,' said Helen.

'Was it closing time?' said Guy, with a voice not quite confident enough for the question.

'Shut up, Guy. This boy came up to me when I was waiting to get served and said, "Now Helen, I used to mend your dad's tractors." He was quite drunk. I thought, well—how can a girl refuse?'

'It'd be Phil Cudlipp.'

'He was called Phil. Was there only one person who mended them?'

'No, but there's only one bloke in Yorkshire who thinks telling you he mended your dad's tractors is a chat-up line. What did you say to him?'

'I asked him which ones he mended. He said he thought it was the Ford and the Leyland, and I said he couldn't have made a very good job of them because they were always breaking down.'

'That Ford's never broken down much.'

'Well I didn't actually know if they did. I was hoping he'd go and find another girl whose dad's machinery he'd worked on.'

'Did he?'

'No. He apologized. I said it didn't matter. Anyway, I've come to help, what shall I do?'

'Hay in t' barn needs sorting out,' said Guy with a slight nervousness in his voice.

'Oh *good*,' she said.

*   *   *

At the bottom of the fat, slumping stack in the barn where I had cleaned the pigs last weekend, the hay bales were thirty years old, brought with us from Marwood when we moved here. New bales of dry grasses, wildflowers and weeds had been added every year, and on many of the older bales that had not been used the twine had rotted or been chewed through by rats. We had to sort it to see which bales were intact, and which needed to be piled up and re-baled for selling.

The stack was unsteady because as the hay had dried over the years, the bales had contracted and buckled. Guy told us to wait at the bottom while he climbed up to pull bales down from the top. Helen and I picked at those that had fallen to the ground. Weak shafts of light shone through the holes in the roof and the slits in the wall, and we looked up at twigs and seed tufts rotating slowly in the sunlight like tiny broken birds.

'Don't fall, Guy,' said Helen.

'Fall!' he said, up in the green-black gloom. He made it sound as though falling was something only children needed to worry about. 'Don't *you* get assaulted by a rat.'

'Thanks,' she said.

'Don't worry. I'll be able to hit it with a pitchfork from here.'

'How nice it is to be part of a loving family where your brother forks rats for you!'

'In a way, maybe it is,' I said, but she stared at me and at Guy, and blankly blinked.

'In a way, maybe. And in a way I am suddenly remembering why I live in town.'

'Do you ever miss living in the country?' I asked.

'Not now. I like being able to walk out and get things,' she replied, hoiking a bale away from the stack. 'Although having said that, I do often think that I'd like to run a donkey sanctuary.'

'Do you want to make it a pig sanctuary?' called Guy.

Helen, put off the stack by the suspicion of rats, began taking some of the hay that burst loose and giving it to the pigs, and as they tossed it the dust swirled above their heads and powdered their pink faces like coarse black flour. The barn filled with a swishy rustling sound like the opening of Christmas presents, and the rising black clouds of seed shells, splinters and awns pricked our eye-rims and choked us.

For a while we rested, and spat clots of black seedy spit into the muck on the floor. Guy pushed the flat of his hand against each nostril in turn, and rifled snot into the muck.

'Charming, Guy,' said Helen.

'It's my barn,' he replied.

We fell to the work again, panting shallowly in a thick mess that felt like warm, seedy ashes. In the door's grey-gold rectangle of light, Dad appeared, and for a moment I felt as if we were three children again. We spent most summers of our childhoods like this, with him in charge, Guy deputizing, and me and Helen lugging straw across rasping stubble fields.

'Hello, Dad,' I said.

'Eyup,' he said. 'Can you all come, quick? There's a pig in Major Twist's garden.'

Tea and Pesticide

Next door to Rose Farm, separated from the farmyard only by a patchy no man's land of shrubs and bushes, stood a large, square brick house with the best-kept garden in Sowthistle.

In this house live Major and Mrs Twist, a retired army couple who moved to Sowthistle from the south of England in the 1970s. They are a precise, courteous and public-minded pair, active on the committees of the parish church and a local village show. Tending to the garden is their chief relaxation, and a source of considerable, and justified, pride. The Twists' lawn is stately-home pristine, their weedless, geometrically perfect flower beds full of unusual and brilliant plants, their antique stone sundial juxtaposed perfectly with the bank of ornamental grasses. Just setting foot on the lawn is enough to make you feel elevated above the untidy chores of day-to-day life; it is the sort of garden I used to imagine Mrs Hirst in, discussing politics with poets and her admirers.

The drawback, of course, was its location next to our yard. One of the flowery borders was overlooked by my dad's muck-cart, and this presented a particular problem. When we were herding young pigs from one shed to another, we moved along holding long plywood boards against the ground to stop them running past us. If you watched the pigs closely, you could usually anticipate any about to make a break for freedom, and head them off by either moving the board, or in extreme cases throwing it so that it landed in front of their snout and scared them into doubling back. However, if they went underneath the muck-cart they were away. We couldn't follow them there, and so we had to try to get around the back of it, hoping we made it before they realized that if they carried on through the bushes and shrubs, and then across the flowery border, they had an escape route into the most inviting and tasty little landscape a pig could dream of.

As a child I had wondered why neither my dad nor Major Twist had put up a fence, and I wondered again now as I ran with my brother and sister from the old barn to join my parents, Mal and Major Twist on the Major's lawn. They were surrounding a panting, foot-high porker whose little hooves had left indents the size of chestnuts across the grass. The human faces concentrated hard on the pig. The pig, looking slightly stunned, concentrated back.

'Reinforcements on the flank!' cried the Major, who loved a military metaphor.

'Brilliant,' said Helen. 'Chasing pigs around next door's garden again. The sweet memories of childhood.'

'Right, you little bastard,' said Guy. His eyes fixed on the pig, and my mum's fixed sternly on him, unsure of how the swearing rules operated on foreign territory. Suddenly Guy lunged for the pig's back leg, missed, and sent it scuttling off towards the gap between me and Major Twist. The Major snatched at empty air and I dived to my left, missed the animal and knocked the edge off a

105

flower bed with my knee. Seeing the pig break through the circle and head for the gate, my dad tossed his board ahead of it. The pig skidded to a halt, then jackknifed back past Mal. Mal grabbed, but his hands came up empty. Deep in his belly, he growled.

The pig picked its way through the grasses and then paused, panting again, in front of the conservatory, where it deposited a sloppy, steaming stream of turds.

'Calm down!' my mum said to it.

I noticed Guy nip back into the farmyard.

The pig calmed down, its panting growing slower. We closed in around it. I sprang forward and grasped its back leg, which is usually the best place to grab a pig because the crook of the knee is easy to get hold of. This is not true, however, if the leg has been lubricated by sweat and liquid excrement; the pig slipped away and then went past my dad, who in lurching to reach it almost collided with the sundial.

There was a fleeting look of terror on my dad's face as he realized he had just missed what he assumed to be an expensive antique, but Major Twist was enjoying the chase. 'Six men including a trained soldier to hunt him down!' he boomed, fringe flopping into his glittering eyes. 'We could do with a few pigs like this in Her Majesty's Forces!'

'Yeah, well, it's all right, t' SAS is here now.' Guy came snarling back into the garden carrying more boards, and accompanied by Karl. I might not have recognized Karl straight away but for the mild swagger and the way that under the thick, dark moustache a smile flashed like someone catching sunlight with a knife.

'Now, Pauline. Gordon. Mal. Helen. Major Twist,' he said, adding, when he noticed me, 'Bloody hell, you're here, are you?'

'IN THAT CORNER!' shouted Guy, who was advancing on the fugitive with a board close to the ground, catching at the shrubbery as he passed. This time the pig headed into an angle of conservatory wall and thick hedge. We closed in tight. It turned and zipped for the gap between the board and Karl, but Helen planted a foot down to deflect it off course, and Karl dropped deftly to his right and grabbed the pig's left back leg with both hands. He passed the pig to my dad, who apologized to Major Twist for the damaged garden, and then carried it back into the farmyard, with us following him in a line.

*   *   *

Back in the yard, Karl told us that he had heard about the sale and come to help. He told Mum and Dad about his three children, and laughed at me for not being able to catch the pig. As we lifted some saleable metal gates from their hinges, he told my dad that the buyers had cut the orders from his farm, and the boss was talking about sacking someone. He said something about it being cheaper to bring in pigs from the Netherlands, something to do with new currencies and the strong pound, and different interpretations of animal welfare laws. What baffled everyone at his place, he said, were the economics that meant British food was ending up in shops on the other side of the world while our shops were buying the same sort of food from abroad.

Later, Helen went in to cook the evening meal and Mum made mugs of tea and brought them to the workshop, where Mal, Guy, Karl, my dad and I had gathered, leaning stiffly against the big iron workbench and the breezeblock walls. My mum placed the tray on a small, empty plastic herbicide drum that I had dragged out with some clutter from the back of the small shed.

'Where've you got that from?' asked my dad, mystified as to how his mental inventory of the yard could have missed this single old five-gallon drum. 'I think they've banned that spray now, tha knows. We used to mix it in t' bloody kitchen sink!'

'That explains a lot,' said Mal. Karl brandished his smile, and Guy looked uninterested.

'Well, we did though, didn't we, Richard?'

Yes.' I remembered liking the unnatural, sulphury-plastic smells of the sprays as I made them into solutions in buckets placed in the sink. After I mixed them, I carried the buckets outside for my dad to pour into the tractor-mounted sprayer.

Like the half-dozen or so different herbicides, fungicides, pesticides and fertilizers we applied to crops in the 1970s and 1980s, the one once contained in the old drum was supplied to us by a strong-jawed young agronomist called Nick, who travelled the area in his Nissan Patrol selling new miracle liquids and powders with exciting names like Commando, Dagger and Stomp. Nick was one of many agricultural college graduates who had worked for grain merchants and realized that the high prices farmers were now getting for their cereal crops meant they were able to invest in new yield-boosting chemicals. These farmers needed advice, and men like Nick set up their own companies to pass on the knowledge supplied by colleges and the chemical manufacturers. Nick called by every so often, had a look at the crops, and told my dad what he could buy to get rid of the pests, weeds and diseases that affected them. Sometimes he left booklets published by chemical companies, telling you what to say to people who objected to pesticide use.

'There's no end of t' sprays that they used to come round and tell you, "Oh yes, it's completely safe, can't possibly do any harm" and all that, that they've banned now.' The subject of pesticides seemed to have captured my dad's imagination. 'We used to slop them about like they were water and mix 'em in t' kitchen, and now they say they were bloody poison! It's a wonder we're not all dead.'

Lots of farmers admit privately that the information about early sprays was unreliable, and many know people who have suffered respiratory and skin diseases as a result. The problem is that if you put that point to them, quite a few think you are a Green, and therefore against them, and therefore someone against whom they have to defend themselves.

'They've got rid of ever so much, tha knows, t' sprays,' he went on. He was looking at me, but it seemed that in a way he was also talking to himself. 'You don't even have so many nettles now, because they spray them all off. It's like flowers. There were ever so many different kinds up t' lane when we came here, and there's half

109

of them gone.'

I was surprised by my dad's gloomy, frank observations. After all, some of those sprays had been applied by us. Well, by him, Karl and Guy: I was only allowed to mix them. 'Didn't you know, though?'

'What, wi' plants and birds and that?' He inhaled and exhaled deeply, and studied his hands. 'Not when people started wi' sprays—I don't think anyone had any idea. All you could think of when t' first one came out were that it got rid of your thistles and docks. Loukin' thistles and docks is a balls-aching job tha knows, and if tha 'ad 'em bad, nobody wanted to come in t' gangs to pull 'em up, and then they'd smother t' crops. Thistles are t' worst, because they seed so much.'

Mal swung his head in sympathy. 'Thistles is a bastard,' he said.

'I remember down at Marwood there was a feller who didn't louk properly, and me and my dad used to go cut his corn for him, and some parts we just didn't bother to cut at all, cos there were more thistles than corn. Tha'd get nowt out of it, and when tha came to stack thy sheaves, tha'd have thistle pins all up thy bloody arms, and they'd be red raw by t' time tha went home. So tha can imagine when we got t' sprays, we just thought they were marvellous. And in them days tha didn't question science and that like people do now . . . well, some maybe did, but nobody thought of what it were doing to t' birds and . . . It took a long time afore anybody realized. I don't think they tested them right.'

'Somebody near us, his wife got took bad with shakes and her skin all blistered up from sheep

110

dip,' said Karl. 'Right bloody mess.'

'But why did people carry on then, if they knew they were poison?' I asked.

My dad sat thinking, dangling his empty tea mug from the one finger he could fit in the handle. 'I think there was a lot of talk that they were being made safer, and . . .' he trailed off. 'Everybody'd got hooked into using 'em . . . Tha knows when tha's making a big profit, it can make thee greedy. When farming were good in t' Seventies and Eighties, all anybody could think of was how to get more and more. It's what we all thought we should do. But as time's gone on and prices have got tighter, a lot have said they think it costs more in spray and fertilizer to get an extra ton than they get back for that ton, so I think they're not spraying like they used to.'

As Dad spoke I noticed Guy's expression darkening like a sky filling with rain clouds. Looking irritated, he stood up from the wall and strode off purposefully with a muck-fork. That broke the spell: Mal and Karl straightened their backs and placed their mugs on the tray, and my dad flicked the last cool half-inch of his tea across the straw and stood up.

'A lot of people in London seem to be buying organic stuff,' I said.

'Oh, aye,' said Mal. 'Tha's one o' them, is tha?'

My dad gave me a look. "S dear though, in't it?' he said. 'I can't see how a woman wi' a family'll pay one pound ten for a loaf if she can get it for a quid.'

'I would,' I said.

'Aye, but tha's a good job and no family. If tha's not much money, tha's to save t' ten pences.'

'They could give people a choice and see how it goes.'

'Aye, but I think they'd have to get used to it not being perfect any more. I think folks is used to apples being all shiny and round and t' same sizes, and they'll not be if tha puts nowt on 'em, like. I reckon folks today think if summat's natural it's perfect, but it in't. Nature's imperfect. Natural's all shapes, like taties.'

*   *   *

Karl told my dad to give him a ring if he wanted a hand at any time, and then drove off in his Mondeo. When I walked back up the yard to find Guy, he was not, as I had expected, riving apart tangles of tools or building the straw-bale circle for parading the animals in on sale day. He was in the sty under the weathervane, vigorously rubbing the neck and talking into the ear of Onkus the boar.

Onkus, the youngest of four boars on the farm, was Guy's favourite. He talked to him with that soft patter that men reserve for animals and their children, working the roots of the pig's ears and rubbing his belly. As Onkus crumpled sighing into the straw, he laughed softly. He did not realize that I was listening, and I walked away to wait for him back in the workshop.

His relationship with the pigs had always been that way, like Dad's: knockabout and matey with the young animals, deeper with the breeding stock, much of which he had reared from infancy, and locker-roomish with boars. In the late 1980s we had an old boar called Champion, whom my dad liked and kept in a back pen of the foldyard after

112

he became too old to couple with sows. When the vet came out he used to say, 'You should get him sold, Gordon, he'll be costing you a fortune in food.'

My dad always replied, 'Aye, we'll have to see about him,' but we never did see, and Champion stayed in the back pen until he died peacefully in his sleep.

The Monogrammed Hammer

My dad had worked out, labouring with ball-point pens on the backs of envelopes and punching numbers into a calculator, that if a builder bought the yard, and the pigs and tackle sold for the prices Bill predicted, he would be able to keep not only the house, but also a tractor, the baler, and the spinney with its shed. That meant he would be able to buy, bale and sell some straw.

'And then there might be something for our Guy, because—' He did not finish this sentence, as he talked to me in the yard the day after we caught the pig on the Twists' lawn, and I did not ask him to.

Apart from the tractor, baler and a few tools, everything that could be sold was to go in the sale. And so for the rest of the month, working through the cold, damp daylight hours into the nights, my dad, mum, brother, sister and I—and, when they had time, Major Twist, Mal, Eileen, Dad's old friend Dickie and an old school friend of mine from the village called John—dismantled what we could of the farm, and carried it piece by piece, in

113

trailers and cars, up into the field near the spinney which looked down to the village.

We brushed down the implements that fitted on the front and back of tractors. We pulled apart piles of old rusty tools with oily green wooden handles, and piled them in trailers for carting away. We took the rest of the gates from their hinges and dragged them to the field, and laid them out in rows with everything else.

Tools grown soft and brown with under-use we put into wooden crates for sale as lots. I poked among them: oil cans, fiddle drills, billhooks, grease guns, hoe blades, cotter pins, chain links and spanners; ornaments, curios, antiques and bric-a-brac. I found objects from my childhood that connected to a past that somehow felt recent and distant at the same time. It suddenly seemed impossible that anyone still alive could have lived in it.

In one box I found an old hammer with the letters NCB engraved on its head. Guy and I had grown up believing that we had a distant, long-dead, semi-aristocratic relative called Nigel Charles Benson, who had had all his tools stamped with his monogram. In reality, this was a joke told to us by our dad; this NCB stood for National Coal Board, the tools having been diverted to him years ago by relatives and friends who worked at Marwood pit. Coal exerted lingering influences on us even when we moved away from the West Riding. Mum and Dad told old stories about the pits, visiting relatives brought new ones, and pals sometimes sorted us out with cheap loads of coal at Christmas. When we got the Volvo, coal brought new, different interrogations from the visiting relatives, or at least from my Cousin Mick, who was something at branch level in the National Union of Mineworkers.

'That's a capitalist car, Pauline,' he said one summer evening, having called in on the way back from the coast. He was stood talking to my mum as she washed it.

'It's a hard-working man's car,' said my mum, who didn't really like Mick.

'I'm hard-working, and I haven't got a car like that.'

'Well . . . save up and get yourself one, then.'

'Come off it, Pauline.'

'Come off it yourself.'

'I an't got capital, have I?'

Later on, my mum gave me a basic explanation of capitalism as we watched *Opportunity Knocks* together. At the end of it, she said that a lot of people in the East Riding knocked miners, but there were as many good men who'd worked down the pit as there ever were around Kirksfield, and I noticed her eyes getting watery.

The following years brought many more arguments about miners and capitalism, most of them ending with my dad looking worried and my mum telling someone off, and then crying a little bit when they left the house. When the NUM went on strike in 1983 my Cousin Alan, who worked at Marwood pit, came to stay with us to help on the farm, and get a break from the tension spreading through South Yorkshire. He had not foreseen the tension and violence spreading between my mother and the feed reps, lorry drivers and neighbours who assumed that we, like most people in the East Riding, especially farmers, were against

115

the strike.

One Thursday night Helen and Guy and I didn't get shouted for our tea at the usual time, and stood instead outside the kitchen door listening while Mum, Dad and Mr Rounding, a stout, ham-faced Methodist who came to take the orders from the pig-feed company, spoke in raised voices. Alan stayed quiet. My mum and Mr Rounding began saying the names Arthur Scargill and Maggie Thatcher so loudly that we could hear them through the thick kitchen door.

'Mum's getting mad,' whispered Helen.

'Serves him right,' I said.

Helen flicked a V at the door. I copied her. Guy shook his head and walked back to the sitting room.

When we finally ate our pork chops, mashed potatoes and gravy, they were lukewarm. Mum looked flushed, and had reddened eyes.

'It isn't about coal, it's about Maggie Thatcher wanting her own back for Edward Heath,' she said. 'Arthur Scargill's walked into a trap.'

'NCB were stockpiling coal nine months before they brought this review thing in,' said Alan.

'She'll do 'em, and then everybody'll have to look out,' said my dad. 'It's all right buying it abroad cos it's cheaper, but at least if you pay folks here that money's going round.'

'I just think it's going to be a very different country,' she replied. 'I don't know about coal, but how do you put a price on places and people? If we're not going to be bothered about that any more, it's like changing t' weights on t' scales.'

Snow Clouds

The Friday before the sale we sorted the pigs into their final lots: sows with litters, weaners, store pigs, gilts, and finally the boars. The main job was trying to make the lots look even, sharing out the smaller, weaker ones among the middle-sized and large ones so that they might fetch a better price, although, given the market, my dad and brother wondered who would want any of them. In the newborn litters, whose mothers might take to piglets not of their own breeding, we swapped some of the small and large piglets around.

At five o'clock that Friday my dad and I drove up to the shed in the spinney to load the last sows. As we climbed out of the car we saw Jack Gemble walking back down the lane with his Jack Russell.

Jack is a retired vermin catcher who lives in a snug, dark bungalow at the bottom of the lane. He has never married, and without a family to mellow a life of snaring and death among rats, bats and weasels, his personality has been dominated by two compulsions: a fascination with natural history and a despairing wonder at the darker aspects of human life. In the animals around Sowthistle, Jack sees an intriguing goodness whose balance he can help maintain; in anything from freak road accidents to men who shoot animals for the thrill of it, he sees a natural but unpredictable evil that can at any point overwhelm us.

These two tendencies in his philosophy coalesce in his conversations about the weather. The older men in Sowthistle love talking about the weather, so much so that once they have begun, they often seem reluctant to stop. When I was younger and out with my dad, my heart sank if he met someone and the subject came up, but that night I found myself not minding as he and Jack readied themselves for a weather conversation. Everything seemed strangely peaceful. As Jack paused at the gate and let his dog run on, the rabbits of chill early evening bobbed in the lane. Over the flat vale to the east, thick white clouds were building in the darkening sky. Over the hills to the west, the sun was setting, making the ploughed and stubble fields glow pinky-brown. The sky had a lot of weather in it.

'Gran' neet,' Jack said.

'It is,' I said.

'Aye,' said Jack, and paused for what seemed like ten minutes. "Ad tha some reean afore?'

'Tha what?' asked Dad.

"Ad tha some reean this afternoon?'

'Aye, a shower.'

'Aye, there was a bit down at Kirksfield. So . . .'

'Aye.'

'Aye.'

'So,' said Dad. There was another long pause. 'It's so bloody cowd for t' time o' year tho', in't it?'

'Aye. Yon looks like snow clouds over there!' Jack nodded towards the clouds, and laughed with incredulous disgust.

'Aye,' I said.

'So,' said Jack.

'Aye,' said Dad.

'Well,' said Jack.

'Aye,' I said.

'Eh?' said Jack.

'What?' I said. 'Oh, nothing . . . nowt . . . just, er . . .'

'Is tha up for a visit?'

'Yes. Just for the weekend.'

'Aye.' Pause. 'Must be a bit different for thee, in't it?'

'Aye, a bit.'

'Aye.' He drew a breath. Longer pause. 'So.'

'Well,' said Dad, 'we shall 'ave t' get on . . .'

'Aye.'

'Aye.'

'Times goes by so fast, doesn't it?' said Jack.

'Oh, aye,' I said.

'It bloody does,' said Dad, pushing through the gap in the hedge towards the shed. 'It'll soon be dark.'

'Next thing we know, it'll be Christmas!' said Jack.

*   *   *

Damp, autumn dusk. Down in the bottom of the valley lights are coming on in the village, and smoke is drifting from chimneys. On the horizon beyond, the monument looms like a grotesque watchtower.

In a stubble field up on the valley side four men are moving with urgency between shadowy piles of random farm tackle—here an old, dented tractor, there a busted and patched trailer, everywhere rusty bouquets of pitchforks and shovels. A tractor bounces roughly across the field, pulling behind it a low trailer bearing an assortment of metal gates, mostly bent, with the red oxide paint worn off

119

them. The tractor's driver stops at the end of a row—there are seven, each with about fifteen piles—leaps down from the cab, and with another two men hauls the gates from the trailer and stands them, propped against one another in twos, each about five yards apart. Finally, as it becomes hard to see in the dark, one of the younger men is given a hose connected to a tap near a shed, and is instructed to hose down two trailers which have been parked up.

Then the other younger man comes bouncing over on a tractor, hitches up a trailer and parks it at the end of a row, then returns to fetch the other one and parks it there too. The men are swallowed in the gathering darkness now, dissolved and gone, and all you can see are the four long creamy beams of the two tractors' lights cutting across an empty field and down the lane into the village.

Then the field is empty but for the black shapes of tools and machines lined in rows, and the rats, rabbits and badgers creeping among them.

The Stick and the Clipboard

In the morning, we rise at seven to bed the pigs with fresh straw so they will look clean. The crowds will arrive at eleven.

At breakfast I suggest to Guy that we should have bought bacon, bread and coffee, and sold sandwiches, but he smiles grimly and says, 'Auctioneers bring their own catering van.'

Sure enough, when we reach the field there is a burger and hot dog caravan already parked in the spinney, powered by a generator that makes a banging noise audible everywhere. Two young men in unclean white overalls are slicing bread-cakes and frying sausage.

At ten when we return to the kitchen, my mum is making cups of coffee and the first cars are gathering outside. Helen has come to take Mum to Scarborough for a few hours, as arranged with my dad last week, after she said she did not want to be here when the strangers were in the yard. Dad's friend Dickie has come with Auntie Eileen. He sits in a corner near the old veneer bureau where my mum keeps the bills and letters, while Auntie Eileen clears and washes pots, and everyone talks about people from the old days—who's dead, and how old their children are, and which empty fields have been built on. Guy tells a story about a farmer who has recently gone bankrupt. He says the farmer's wife has cystic fibrosis, and the man who worked for him is being evicted from his tied cottage. The evicted man has two daughters, eleven and nine. 'We can't complain, really, can we?' he says.

And then it is time. Mum and Helen drive off while Dad and Guy ride up to the field in Dickie's pick-up. John from the village offers me a lift in his Nissan Micra, but as I am getting into the car I remember I have left my jacket in the kitchen, and run back in to get it. The house is quiet and still. As I pass the living room, I see Auntie Eileen standing, her mouth pinched shut, just staring out of the window and down into the yard.

There are cars, Land-Rovers, Fourtraks, pick-ups and vans, most splashed with muck and crusted below the waistline with dry, pale-brown

121

mud, parked along the roadsides near the yard. The lane verges are crammed with them, and there are more in the field—Isuzus, Mitsubishis, Range Rovers, Ford Mavericks—where the burger van bangs and the auctioneers point at the rows.

John parks in a corner of the field, and although the field has not belonged to anyone in my family for almost ten years, as I get out I feel as if I have pulled back the curtains of my flat to find the audience for a country show crowded into the garden. In front of me, slowly walking past, a pair of men, one well over six feet tall with grey hair like ghostly undergrowth, the other no more than five two, with a flat-capped head pulled right down into a worn-out Barbour coat. Striding the other way is a tall, wealthy-looking man in a long oiled mac and a Drizabone hat with two pheasant feathers in its band. To my right, two women in early middle age wearing green Goretex jackets and blue wellingtons smile and nod in a conversation lost in the noise of the generator.

Elsewhere men in caps and boots hunch in clusters, some talking, some prowling the rows, others toeing tyres or boxes of tools. Men in their forties and fifties watch sons clamber over the Ford, the John Deere, the combine harvester, and shake trailer sides checking for firmness. Lads in overalls and rigger boots lope about, and silvery whiskery old gadgers in rough tweed working jackets, rollies hanging on their dry lips, gaze tremulously into the middle distance.

More pick-ups bounce into the field. More toes prod tyres and boxes. Eyebrows rise and fall, mouths murmur and bite bacon butties, and raw red hands rub against the cold. There are greetings

122

and askings after family, and talk about work and the prospects of rain. A sharp wind whips in intermittently, and when it lulls, a tang of cigarettes and frying onions distils on the brawny autumn air.

I look out across the hills, and down over the plain towards Kirksfield. I feel as if I should be able to tell that something awful is happening here; as if there should be an appalled stillness, with the trees quiet and all birds respectfully roosting in them. But the birds are in flight, wheeling in a cold, clear blue sky, and below them tractors are moving indifferently through the fields. Down in the village, the wind rags the smoke out of chimneys, and children play on mountain bikes. On the roads, cars and trucks pass through the landscape as smoothly as schooners through a calm sea.

When Bill Warburton's van bounces and bumps into the field, the low excited apprehension rises like a fattening gas flame. The master of today's ceremonies, Bill is a medium-sized, efficient-looking man with a toothy smile. As he gets out of his van and strides over to my dad, he nods discreetly at friends and swings in his left hand a clipboard and in his right a short ashplant. The two men put their heads down, fold their arms, and confer; I feel a sort of suspended panic, and want to stride over to be beside my dad, but I daren't. I notice how serene he looks.

'Deep in thought, lad—don't wear yourself out.' The familiar, moustachioed voice at my shoulder makes me breathe properly again. It is Karl, looking mildly cross because that is how he looks when he feels miserable.

123

'Not much of a laugh, is it?' I say.

'Fuckin' in't.'

We watch my dad talking to Bill Warburton.

'You demonstrating t' tackle?' he asks me, smiling.

'Should I have brought my outfit?'

'I thought that was it.'

We look at each other and make little grimacey intakes of breath. Then he seems to get disgusted at our small talk. He look as if he wants to hit someone.

'I'm fucking choked up. I can't believe Gordon. If it were me I'd be—I wouldn't be here, I'm telling you.'

'I know,' I say. 'I don't know what he'll do, Karl.'

'I know. Everybody's going t' same way, like. It's all this fucking Dutch pork they're bringing in.'

*   *   *

They begin selling at five past eleven. Starting at the top of the row furthest from the gate, the auctioneer works down the field, amid a sedate scrum of people shuffling from box of ploughshares to cultivator to bundle of shovels. Boots tear the soft ground, and by the time they reach the second row they are tramping through sludge. I wander about trying to look as if I'm doing something, and hear the auctioneer bang down his stick to sell the gates for eight pounds apiece.

He knocks down the combine at lunchtime, and that is the last thing. Next is the yard.

My dad comes over and tells me to go home ahead of everyone, to warn Auntie Eileen they are

124

coming, and then to wait in the yard near the show ring.

Back at the house, Mum's friend Myrtle is talking to Auntie Eileen, and wiping her country wind-worn eyes with a little lacy handkerchief.

'Eyup, love,' says Auntie Eileen. 'Is your dad all right?'

'He seems to be.'

She raises her eyebrows a millimetre, and smiles.

Crowds of milling men soon fill the yard and push into every corner looking for cheap treasures. They jostle to get a look in the sties and sheds. The autumn light seems bronze and close, full of shadows; there is the cigarette smoke again, and the faint mist of dust in the air from the churning of the fresh straw and hay we had put in that morning.

Guy and I push through the crowds to shoo the pigs in and out of the ring for the auctioneer, giddily lost in our work, laughing with nerves and slight hysteria. The whole spectacle feels so unreal it is almost funny.

In the slump of mid-afternoon, the sale loses its momentum. Bill discovers lots he thinks he has already sold. Assistants call him back to feed trolleys, buckets, the planks that once covered the grain pit. My dad moves round with the auctioneer, occasionally corroborating or correcting something from the sheet of word-processed details. He looks impassive, even cheery. The unfamiliar tobacco smoke, the rattle of the strangers' boots in the sludge grow banal, and I feel numb. I elbow into the crowd for a bit, and see the man sell Onkus: 'Now then, one boar, two years, excellent condition, you can see: who'll start me at three hundred?'

The boar is bought by a bluff, blondish man in a brown-and-white check shirt. He looks OK, but not like the sort of man to give his boars names like Onkus or Champion. But then Guy doesn't look like that sort of man either.

Then they come to a small, makeshift pen with the two black Berkshire-cross sows Double and Trouble. They have come from weird breeding throwbacks, and have a sort of working-pet status.

'These the ones, Gordon?' Bill asks my dad, who is hard by him.

My dad nods his head and says, 'Aye, that's 'em.'

I look at Guy, and Guy shrugs.

'Right, these not for sale!' calls Bill. 'Next, then! Ten store pigs, very good condition—'

*   *   *

When it was over, we sat in the kitchen with the plastic wall-clock ticking, not saying anything, just slurping mugs of tea. There was me and Guy, Bill Warburton, Dickie, Eileen and my dad himself, who was just sitting silent, his cap on the table, his eyes staring unseeing at the skirting board, one hand cradling the other. He sighed heavily, and I saw Bill look at him.

Outside the kitchen window, the sky had clouded over, and the cool sunshine was turning to the underwater shadow-light you get on late October afternoons when the sun is slanting in under dense clouds, its brightness trapped in narrow beams, unable to rise and spread. In the garden shadows were measuring out the remnants

126

of day. A pair of sparrows lighted on the nesting-box lid, glanced in through the window, and flew off again.

At five o'clock, we heard the sound of a car stopping, the slam of two doors, and then murmuring voices on the path. Mum and Helen walked past the window. When Mum came into the kitchen and saw my dad, she took a sharp breath, and went over to him and took his head in her hands and lifted it up and kissed him on the forehead. Then she wrapped her arms around him as he sat there, and he gave a very heavy, raspy sigh and sank against her and everything seemed to freeze as the clock kept ticking. Then there were only her sobs, and the tiny pats of his tears falling on the old muddy carpet at his feet.

Goodbye Onkus

Men with cars and trailers called to collect the pigs they had bought, and Guy and I went out to help them. I asked him if they had a form or something to prove how many pigs they could take.

'No,' he said, uninterestedly.

'What's to stop them taking more than they paid for, then?'

'Nowt, I suppose.'

'Do they ever, do you think?'

'No. You get people rustling pigs out of fields, though.'

'Oh. I don't remember people doing things like that when I lived here.'

'Not many people had pigs in fields when you

lived here. Free-range pigs are trendy now.'

'But why shouldn't people try it on when they come to collect pigs, like now?'

He shrugged, clearly bored by our conversation. 'It's just something you don't do.'

'Just sort of a code of honour, isn't it?'

'Yes, if you like. Plus you'd always be able to find somebody if you needed to sort 'em out.'

The cars and little trucks kept coming until about ten o'clock.

Mum, Dad, Helen, Guy and I sat about in the kitchen, and talked about who had been at the sale, and how much money everything had made. My dad said Bill thought the sale would make enough to pay off the debts.

I woke up in the middle of the night, and heard my dad talking confusedly in his sleep.

*   *   *

Most of the pigs were still there by noon the next day, and so we kept feeding them. Guy said it was a business tactic: the buyers could get away with leaving the pigs here for a few days, and they knew that they'd get fed, which meant they would save ten or twenty quid on food. Early in the afternoon, as we started brushing out the sties and sweeping the shed floors for the last time, a farmer arrived in a blue Land-Rover with an aluminium car-trailer, and said he'd come for the young boar. Guy showed him where to reverse, waved him back, and went into the pen.

'Come on, Onk.' He nudged Onkus's haunches with his boot to make him get up, and ushered him to the door. The Lincolnshire farmer took from inside the Land-Rover an inch-wide stick bearing the logo of a national pig-breeding company, and whacked Onkus across the back, making the pig bolt nervily into the trailer. The farmer quickly swung the gates shut, latched them together, and then lifted up the sprung door.

'Right then, ta,' he said, wiping dirt from his hands on a wall.

'Ta,' said Guy.

As the Land-Rover started to move, Guy was already walking away silently. When it pulled out of the yard, he glanced back at it over his shoulder.

'You all right?' I said.

'Yep.' He closed the road gate. He looked even less in the mood for a conversation than he usually did, which was saying something.

'At least you're getting through it,' I said.

'Mmm.'

'You can have a rest soon.'

There was just a faint snort in reply to that. He pushed a shed door until it latched, and then he turned to me and said, 'What you going to do, then?'

'Go back, I suppose.'

He tilted his chin upwards by a millimetre, raised his eyebrows and nodded.

The Cat and the Blackbird

I had booked three days off work, and already stayed for four. On the fifth, my boss called me about some impending meetings.

'I'm coming back tonight,' I told him. 'I'm not

sure I'm in the right frame of mind, to be honest, but I'll be in tomorrow morning.' I was looking out of the bedroom window into the yard. There were now just a dozen sows left, and most of the sties were empty.

'Must've been pretty rough,' he said.

'Well, you know. That's not what I meant actually, but . . .'

'It's great that you've spent time away from London, though. It gives you sort of a proper perspective on stuff, doesn't it?'

Guy stalked across the yard, a pig-board under his arm and a cat prancing along after him.

'You could say that,' I said.

*   *   *

After tea I stowed my bags in my hire car's boot and turned to hug my mum and then my dad. Guy hung back. As I started the car he just said, 'See you', and then went back into the house.

I turned on to the road leading south to the motorway, but once I was out of sight of the village I pulled into a field gate, turned off the engine, and just sat there in the darkness. Feeling the back of the car tugging in the slipstream of lorries as they whooshed past behind me, I stared out over the black field, and thought about nothing.

Eventually I fired up the engine, reversed back out of the gateway and set off again. I drove in silence through the scattered, sodium-lit villages of the Wolds, and then dropped down into busier M62 hinterlands where the houses had painted wooden signs outside advertising logs, eggs, carrots, honey or sheepskin rugs. Then on through the motorway night, past service stations and new warehouses and distribution depots, dozens of vast crinkly tin sheds decorated with global gobbledegook names: IKEA, Rittall, Plastex, Uniq. I stopped at a Welcome Break to buy drinks, and as I drove on, sucking sour coffee through a plastic cup lid, I began thinking about the two pigs that had been saved. It struck me that in the past, when my dad told me to look after myself and to worry less, he was not as I thought at the time, trying to make me selfish, but to make me invulnerable; perhaps to make me less like him, because he knew his own areas of weakness where he could be hurt. I thought about Guy and Onkus, and then about both his and my dad's relationship with their animals. I had often thought about this in the past, because when I talked to vegetarians I sometimes tried to explain that to me, my family seemed more human than the bare facts would suggest. I do not think I ever convinced anyone about this; usually I just sounded defensive. After all, how could you possibly claim an affection between men and the animals they bred to kill?

I felt that I understood it, although I could never explain it, even to myself. Guy would just say, 'That's how it is—if someone weren't going to eat them, I'd never get to look after them', and that sounded like a brutalized feeling, a sensitivity warped, deformed or severed, if you had never seen him talking into a boar's ear, or looking over his shoulder at a trailer carrying one of his pigs out of the yard. I remembered visiting home one Christmas many years ago, coming into the kitchen at about nine in the morning, and finding Guy— who would have been about sixteen at the time—in

131

his work clothes, sitting at the table with his hands covering his face.

I asked him what was wrong. He ignored me. I looked at Mum, and she ignored me as well.

'Guy?' I said.

He didn't move.

'What's up?'

'Nowt!' He flung his hands down and pushed himself back from the table. 'Nowt!' he said. 'Nowt's up!'

He didn't look at anyone, but just spat in a cursing voice, 'Christ! Can't anybody leave me alone?' and stormed out of the house, banging the door behind him.

'Guy!' I shouted after him, but it seemed best to let him go.

'What's up with him?' I asked Mum.

'His cat's had his blackbird. T' blackbird comes and sits on t' weathervane when he goes and feeds his pigs in a morning, and he always talks to it when he goes out. He found it dead this morning. Cat must have had it, and it's upset him, but he'll not say owt about it.'

Looking back on that morning, I wondered what Guy's upset was really about. Grief is always a ravel of briars too tight to be comprehended when you are caught up in it. Perhaps Guy's sadness was to do with the insoluble, volatile algebra of loving a creature that has killed another creature you loved. Or the giddy apprehension that the natural world is not simply cruel and unfair but, in the end, just infinitely indifferent, to us and to itself.

Leicester Forest East, Milton Keynes, London Gateway. The names of corporations faded into those of leisure facilities and theme parks: Johnsen

Diversey, Alton Towers, Tesco, Mattel, The American Adventure. As the lit-up glass and concrete buildings thickened around me, I passed a neon sign saying 'Nissan welcomes you to London'. The sign, with its too-small and too-dim letters, looked underwhelming and sad, but it made Sowthistle and my family and the black field suddenly feel very far away.

A Small Wall

If, in the winter months which came in on the tail of the last St Ledger horse, I had known the things that I learned after the sale of Rose Farm that year, I would have resigned from my job straight away and gone back to stay in Sowthistle for a good length of time—long enough, at the very least, to realize that places are really only ever collections of people, and not repositories of answers and magic.

However, as it was I did not go back for several weeks. One reason for this was that the company I worked for was bought by a large multinational media organization. My new managers were of the modern school, and organized meetings at which they wore charcoal suits with open-necked shirts, and used modern phrases like 'blue-skying' and 'media-neutrality'. We didn't get on very well, and after a few weeks they offered me a redundancy deal, which I took, with as my future plan only the vague idea that I did not want to work in an office any more.

Another reason was that I met a new girlfriend,

a newspaper journalist called Anne. I had ended a relationship with the usual evasiveness and difficulty several months before the sale, and now I decided to try to make this one work. This was fine until Anne said she wanted to meet my mum and dad, and to see the farm and the village. It was only when she asked me that I realized how important it was to me that she liked them. I told her that it was too strange just at the moment, but promised that we would go. The truth, which I could not explain to her or myself, was that I wanted her to see Rose Farm, Sowthistle and my family the way I remembered them. What I did not tell her was that with the farm sold, my dad quiet and Guy reluctant to talk about anything, the life that I had used to explain myself to myself had gone. When I did think about Rose Farm, or Sowthistle, or my family, it was mostly at off-guard moments: on Sunday mornings watching *Countryfile*, when I would sometimes get a lump in my throat and have to look away from Anne as she sat next to me on the sofa, or coming across a farmers' market where someone was selling free-range pork.

I found it hard to settle again. I became a freelance writer, and took any trip that was offered. I flew to Stuttgart to cover a sportswear story, to Stockholm to write about a drinks company, to obscure cities in the US to interview pop groups. In taxis, aeroplanes and lounges, eating sachets of salted peanuts and stale bread rolls, or at home unpacking, washing clothes and packing for the next trip, I felt strangely at peace because I didn't have to think about anything. Anne travelled a lot too, so we made the most of seeing each other when we were both in London. When I was at home on my own, I wrote up the stories, and went to the pub, and phoned Rose Farm and Helen once a week.

My mum took a job at a café behind a petrol station in Northburn, the next village along the York road. My dad worked for Jim Croskill on days when he needed extra men, and got work gardening on a nearby estate. Guy went to Jim's most days, and when the workload was light he went to Brawston's, a large farm on the high Wolds which had a potato-processing plant, to haul their potato-peeling mash to farms where it was used for livestock feed.

*   *   *

When I did visit Sowthistle again, on a cold, bright weekend in winter, the lane-gate was screened off with temporary steel fencing, and the path that used to connect the house to the yard was bisected by a six-foot-high brick wall. The builder who had bought the yard and buildings had taken possession, and begun moving in equipment. Behind the fencing, plastic buckets and lengths of blue corrugated water pipe skittered around in the light wind. Dandelions, dock leaves, thistles and moss were growing in the ground, and in the walls of the brick sheds. The electricity poles had been stripped of wire, the doors removed from the barns, and windows patched with white polythene fertilizer sacks.

When I let myself in—it was afternoon, and everyone was at work—I went up to my old bedroom and looked down at the yard, and saw

135

that somehow the weathervane had been damaged: it was missing its west and south arrows, as well as the little copper Viking boat. I felt a pang when I noticed this, but the feeling was not one of sadness so much as numb surprise. The walls and the weed-sprouting buildings had the reality only of images on a cinema screen. Briefly I overlaid images of Guy, Helen and me riding on the backs of sows when we were small; Karl letting down the tyres of Mal's bicycle; me carrying spray concentrate from the kitchen to my dad at the sprayer; my mum carrying kettles of boiling water through the snow to thaw frozen pipes in winter. The images did not feel as if they belonged there any more though. I sat down on my bed and thought.

We never really own anything.

Nor do we ever learn any ways to cope when we lose those things that we love. It is just that as adults we carry on as if we do, because that way we do not distress those who love us, do not dishonour our contracts, do not bore our friends and neighbours.

Still, I thought, my mum, dad and brother will just get on with it now. If you were robust like them, problems pearled up and slid off the outside of you like raindrops sliding off feathers. The unpleasant events were over. Within a season or two, wouldn't life here have new predictability and assurance about it? I thought so, but as I was about to discover, not all unpleasant events do slide off the outside of robust people. Some have a way of passing through to the inside, where they continue unfolding long after most people have forgotten them.

Wonderful Dr Wilkinson

That evening me and Mum were putting hot paper-wrapped bundles of food from Sowthistle's fish-and-chip shop into the Aga for warming when Dad and Guy came in from potato picking at Jim's. All the rain in the autumn had pushed the potato harvest back that year, and they had been working in dry and bitter winds. Buttoned and zipped layers of thermal underwear, fleece and overall made them look twice as wide as they usually did, and there was fine soil in the cold crimson creases at their eyes.

Guy went to the sink and turned on the hot water tap, sending clouds of steam up as he scrubbed at his hands with a nail brush. Waiting his turn, my dad clasped the radiator to heat his hands. When they began to burn he turned them to cook the backs. Mum unrolled and unwrapped fish, sausages, pies, chips and peas. 'Did you get much done?' she asked Dad.

I noticed that he seemed to hold back from replying, almost shy in our presence.

Guy said, 'It's been a bast—' but then seeing Mum lift her eyebrows he checked himself and began again. 'It's too wet. Mud's coming up t' harvester in big hosses' 'eads, and you can't break it to get taties out. It wants some more dry weather yet. You wouldn't believe t' ruts in t' gate-holes.'

'I would,' she said. 'I've done enough taties in my time, you know. Been there, done it, seen the T-shirt.'

'It's *got* the T-shirt.'

137

'Which one?'

'The phrase is "been there, done it, got the T-shirt". Pass me t' vinegar, will you, Richard?'

'You do your taties, sunshine, and I'll do t' catchphrases. And don't eat your tea so fast, you'll get indigestion,' she said.

'Whatever.' Defeated, he turned to me. 'Don't you fancy a bit of tatie-ing then, or is it too cold for you?'

'Not really, thanks.'

'Might it be a bit hard for you wi' all us lot out in all that mud?'

There was no answer to this sort of question, so I tried to make a joke of it. 'Maybe it could be an interesting bonding experience for me.'

'Bonding?' said my mum.

'It's a yuppie word,' said Guy. 'But I'm not bonding with anybody. I like to stay in my nice warm tractor cab, thank you very much.'

'How do you communicate with people, then?' she asked.

Chewing a mouthful of fish and peas, and sticking his fork into a wedge of chips, he pulled his mobile phone from his trouser pocket and held it up in the air.

'Mobile phones!' she said. 'They're turning us into robots.'

Guy rolled his eyes, and dropped fish skin for the cats. The robot reference prompted another idea for him. 'Tell you what, I was listening to Radio 1 in my tractor t' other day, and Jo Wiley was going on about how she'd been stuck behind a tractor and how it was all like backwards in t' country and all that, and I said to her, "Piss off!" There's tractors—sorry Mum, I was annoyed—

there's tractors that'll have more technology in 'em than her studio! That computer in my tractor at Jim's, you can link it to a satellite to tell you where you're ploughing now, you know. Even you would've been able to drive it, Rich.'

'Well, I think that's sad,' said Mum.

'It's progress, Mother.'

My dad's knife and fork clinked as he laid them on his empty plate. As we had been talking, he had been steadily eating, his uninterested stare averted from us. He looked like a man who would rather be anywhere else than where he was, but was unsure of where to go.

'I taped a cowboy,' my mum said, turning to him to take his plate. 'Do you want to watch it? I think it's Jimmy Stewart.'

'I'm not bothered,' he said. 'Can do.'

'I think it's that one where he's a sheriff.'

My mum taped every Western that was shown on television, and she and my dad always watched them together regardless of how many times they had seen them before. But now he just sighed and said, almost to himself, 'Well, we've seen 'em all, anyroad. You always know how it's going to end.'

Mum did not say anything, and just cleared away the dishes.

*　　　*　　　*

On Saturday and Sunday, Dad and Guy drove back to Jim's in Guy's Fourtrak. Mum did not work at the café at weekends, and so after breakfast we sat in the kitchen drinking coffee and talking.

'Do you think Dad's all right, Mum?' I asked

her on Sunday.

'I'm hoping he will be now. I made him go to the doctor.'

I thought I must have misheard her.

'I mean Dr Wilkinson at t' surgery. Dr Clough's retired.'

'What for?'

'Well t' other morning it scared me,' she said. 'He'd hardly said a word all week, and it got to Friday and he just sat there and stared, and I just felt like he wasn't with me at all. I thought—ooh, you know, I hope he doesn't do something daft, or . . . He just looked like he was going to break down, Richard, so I thought to myself, "Right, Pauline: you're going to have to do something here." And so I said, "Right, Gordon, go and get your jacket and your smart trousers on right now, because I'm ringing up and I'm taking you to t' doctor. *Now.*"

'He just looked up at me and said, "Please don't make me go." But I just said, "Gordon, this is no way to carry on. We've still got our health, and we've still got ourselves. Nobody can take that away from us, but we have to look after it. You're just worn out, and we're going to t' doctor and that's that." He begged me not to ring up, and I thought, you stubborn bugger, you . . . I said I'd ring up to call them out, and he gave in then. He went and got changed, and Dr Wilkinson said we could go to talk to him at t' end of his surgery.

'He was wonderful, Dr Wilkinson. He asked us to tell him what it was about, so I started off explaining it, and then your dad explained a bit, and he said, "You know, there's no shame in this,

140

Gordon, it's depression, and it's just an illness. A lot of men, because they can't see something, they don't think it matters. They don't think how they feel is something they have to look after. But they do have to look after it."

'Anyway, Dr Wilkinson just kept saying, "Don't worry, Gordon, we'll soon get you better." He gave him some tablets and said to come back in a couple of months.'

We sat in silence for a minute.

'You see people our age, we're different to you. Especially fellas. A lot of them think something like depression is like being a bit . . . well, you don't talk about it. So they just sit and brood. It takes a bigger man to admit he's got a problem than to pretend he hasn't, you know.'

'No . . . I mean, yes,' I said.

Cigars

Later that morning, my mum told me a story about Mr Miller, the owner of a large arable farm on the edge of Northburn, who had last year tried to kill himself.

In his seventies, feeling his sense of purpose draining away with his strength and stamina, Mr Miller had one morning sat alone in his kitchen with a shotgun clamped between his knees, its barrel jammed under his chin. When he pulled the trigger, recoil skewed the barrel and the shot sprayed blood, tissue and bone fragments over two walls and the ceiling. The Millers' cleaner found him still alive, called an ambulance, and Hull

Royal Infirmary surgeons saved him. Everyone in the village said that if he'd been thinking straight, he'd have realized a shotgun makes a lousy suicide weapon. Lead shot is not made for killing people: it spreads out when it leaves the gun, and makes a messy, shallow wound.

As all British farmers, and their wives and children, know, suicide rates in the job are high— the fourth highest after doctors, dentists and librarians. I thought about this quite often that winter, as my dad remained quiet and withdrawn from us. In those months, anyone meeting him publicly might have thought he was fine. Even in the house, the parts of him that were husband, father and worker were all still fully present, and he dutifully fulfilled all the expectations that his family had of him. It was just that the substance of his personality seemed to have been stolen, and he seemed to have lost interest in himself. 'I don't mind,' he said one afternoon when my mum suggested a walk up to the spinney to look at Double and Trouble. 'It doesn't make any difference, does it?'

Of course, seen from a distance there had been no great tragedy. He had after all retained a comfortable house, a car, and a family who continued to love him. What had been taken away from him was his idea of his connection to the rest of the world. That, as I realized, can be far harder to replace than houses or cars, especially when you are used to spending much of your time alone. Even the most enduring man or woman can be undone if they lose sight of who and what their lives join them to, or if they come to believe that nothing they do has value to anyone else.

142

I never thought he would do what Mr Miller had done, but I did worry about how he would get back his old sense of connection. In a very strange way this made me feel closer to him, because as well as being the enduring father he now seemed like a friend who shared my, and everyone else's, vulnerabilities. That made me want to make him believe that what he did was valuable, and that the world still wanted to be connected to him, but that was hard. Of course you can *tell* someone that things are going to be fine, and problems are not their fault, but how do you really show it to make them believe it? This was a question I asked myself several times as I visited Sowthistle over that winter.

*   *   *

One night in February Guy and I went out for a pint to the Rose and Crown in Sowthistle. Waiting to order, I noticed on the glass-ringed bar, snucked in between the telephone and a John Smith's ashtray, a small cardboard box with the words 'Rural Stress Network' printed on its side. The box contained small laminated cards. On one side of the cards was a picture of a field with round straw bales in it, and on the other a list of organizations you could call if you were 'at the end of your tether'. I pulled one out and took it back to the table with the pints and pork scratchings.

'Oh, them,' said Guy. 'They had them in this pub just outside Kirksfield. Landlord put 'em on t' bar where people got served and no one took 'em. Then somebody moved 'em round t' corner where no one could see, like, and it emptied, apparently.'

143

Guy did not seem surprised or impressed by this.

'What do you think about that?' I said.

He knew I was expecting him to say people should just pull themselves together, but as people always do when they know what you expect, he said something else.

'I think those cards are good. If people are depressed and it makes them like, you know, down, then they should get help off somebody.'

'Do you?'

'Yeah. It's hard when you have to see your life all wiped out, in't it? Whatever you've done. I don't think anybody should have to go through that. I know there's nowt you can do, but I don't think anyone should have to go through it.'

'No.' We went quiet for a bit, and I ate a pork scratching.

'There was a bloke lived up near Brawston's got laid off and started staying in all t' time and just smoking dope. He lived in this cottage right up on t' high Wolds, and it's real beautiful scenery. You wonder how anybody could get down, but they do.'

'Getting a bit down' was the euphemism for 'depression', a new partner for 'doing something daft'.

'I didn't think you'd notice the scenery,' I said.

'Course I do.' He looked at me with the slight offence you might have if someone asked if you had paid for objects in your possession. 'I love it up on t' high Wolds there when I'm working at Brawston's. If you turn your engine off all you can hear is birds. It's fucking lovely.'

'I've never been up there.'

'I'll take you, if you like.'

144

'OK,' I said. 'Do you want another?'

As I waited to be served, I looked back to see Guy staring thoughtfully into space. He looked as if he was considering our conversation. When I brought the drinks back to the table, he restarted it before I had even sat down properly.

'The thing I think about being down,' he said, 'is that yes, it might help you to talk about it, and tell people your problems and that, but at the end of the day you've still not got any money to pay your bills, and the person you tell might turn round and say, "Well, I've got loads of money", which makes you feel worse. It might just be the money that's worrying you. It might not be a deep psychological thing.'

'No, but then it might be something deeper as well.'

'Yes. I'm not being all, like, anti deep-and-meaningful psychology, I'm just saying.'

'Freud said sometimes a cigar is just a cigar.'

'Did he now?'

'Freud the psychoanalyst, I mean.'

'I know who Freud was.'

'I know you know, I was just saying.'

'Yeah, all right, smartarse,' he said. 'But what's a cigar?'

The Couch

Spring passed into summer. The café where my mum worked grew busier. Dad bought unwanted straw from some Sowthistle farmers, made it into bales, and stored it in the spinney, hoping to sell it on later in the year. In what had been the farmyard, builders laid the foundations for new houses, and stripped out the inner walls and floors of the old barn.

I kept taking work trips, but at times when there was no trip available and Anne was away, I went to stay in Sowthistle. After taking me on the promised Fourtrak drive across the high Wolds, Guy had begun giving me regular Sunday afternoon tours of different parts of the East Riding, and I had come to look forward to them. We would rattle down narrow lanes with swallows swooping in front of us and cow parsley whipping at the windows, and he would point out fields he worked in, and farms he knew, and hamlets that I had never even seen. Sometimes we ended up down on the coast, at Filey or Scarborough or Bridlington, and we would stop and have ice cream, and Guy would tell me what he had been doing at work as we looked at the sea. I loved the warm, green, cat-like ease of those afternoons, and I sometimes daydreamed about them when I was riding on buses, or killing time in over-polished teak-and-marble hotel bars.

For a while, though, I continued to enjoy the anonymity of my work trips. I liked the smooth movement through brightly lit, branded spaces, and I even quite liked interacting with all the modern, tidy hotel people who did not quite seem to focus on you as you were speaking to them. But I think I may have taken too many trips, because one day that summer I returned to London feeling strange, and took what seemed at the time to be a rather extreme decision.

I had been to cover the opening of a European

fashion house's new, architecturally significant flagship store in Tokyo. The four days were crammed with briefings in spectacular rooms, lavish dinners and visits to grand museums with smart young professionals who were very good at making small talk and jokes. Most of them were well-off, smiling and strident people whom it should have been exhilarating to be among, but on the last night we were there, a small thing happened that afterwards I could not get out of my mind.

After a long dinner at which I had sat trying to think of things to say to a French sales director, we went by coach to a fashionable area where someone, somehow knew a nightclub where cool kids were supposed to hang out. Our well-dressed—and drunk—group, with me in the middle of it, pushed down the stairs past some Japanese teenagers who were queuing. The boy and girl on the cash desk said we had to go back and queue, but a man from a national newspaper, who had appointed himself as our leader, pulled out a business card, pushed it at their faces, and said, 'Do you know what this is? Do you understand? We are *from London.*'

The boy and girl looked uncomfortable, but let everyone in. There was a Japanese rap-metal band on stage. People in our party made scathing faces at each other, and most of them left before finishing a drink.

I don't know why, but I kept thinking about that man with his business card, and it made me feel miserable. At Narita Airport, waiting for the flight home, I sat at a departure gate eating a flavourless sandwich from a polystyrene plate, and felt a bleak emptiness slowly settling inside of me that I couldn't shift. I did not understand it, and I felt ashamed that I, with all the privileges of a decent income, friends and a place on a press trip to see an architecturally significant building in Tokyo, should feel miserable in that way, but there it was: I did.

Back in London I told my friend Jennifer, a New Yorker, about the trip and the feeling, and she asked me what my analyst said about it. I said I didn't like the idea of psychoanalysis. I thought it was self-indulgent, and that anyone could figure out how people had screwed them up if they spent long enough thinking about it.

'Man, in New York people would think you were kind of weak for *not* seeing one,' said Jennifer. 'You know, they're just like people who've seen other people going through what you're going through, and have ideas about it.'

I was very susceptible to anyone who had had similar experiences to me and worked out answers to the questions arising from them, so Jennifer's description changed my mind. Once I thought about analysts in this way, going to see one just seemed like renting a new mate.

I chose my analyst from the Yellow Pages, on two principles. First, that they should live in northwest London because that was where Freud had started, and second, that they should have a foreign and if possible old-sounding name because it would be easier to talk to someone from a country other than the United Kingdom. Which is how I ended up spending one evening a fortnight picking at the arms of a leather chair in a study in Golders Green, telling stories about myself, my family, and pigs to an old Hungarian existential psychotherapist from Budapest.

I liked him from the first meeting. He asked me why I had come, and I explained, and then said, 'Look, I think I know what you're going to say: you're going to say it's all to do with guilt and my family. I want you to know that I've already thought this through, and I feel that I already know how it has and hasn't affected me.'

'Well, I am not so interested in guilt in itself,' he said. 'I believe that guilt is like many emotions, a thing your social group teaches you to feel in order to make you loyal. This is the existentialist view, you see. Your group teaches you this thing you call guilt in order that when you are inclined to harm it, you will experience doubt. This keeps the group strong.'

'Oh, right,' I said. 'What about the emotion of love, then?'

'What we call love is complex,' he said. 'But we can look at this in many ways . . .'

'I meant, do you think that your group teaches you the emotion of love as well?'

'In some cases it certainly does, but that is hard to answer because in the society we live in, we have this word "love" which different people use to describe different things. Some people use the word "love" to describe how they feel about someone they think can give them something they want. Some people—perhaps the *same* people, you see—use it to say how they feel about someone they cherish and want to protect . . . If you mean romantic love such as you see in Hollywood movies, then yes, this is definitely something that we learn to believe . . . Often all these feelings and

149

beliefs are mixed together, but we can try to separate them out and to understand them.'

'But it sounds as if you think people don't really feel *anything*—'

'No, of course we do, because we feel something *here*—' he said, and thumped his own chest with a bony yellow fist. 'But then we also have relationships which can make it hard to express those feelings, and then we question what those feelings are. The problem is that our relationships can make us feel worthless and trampled down, and then to make ourselves feel we are not the worst people of all, we trample down somebody else, and then they trample down somebody else, and so it goes on. This is why your friend in Tokyo needed to make kids let him into their nightclub. It is why people start wars and build big statues of themselves.'

'But not everyone does that—'

'Of course not, but you are here because in your own way you feel trampled down, and you want to understand why. People do many different things to cope with this. Sometimes they will do things that actually no one else understands! Because one person might give importance to a thing that another has no interest in at all. A rich person who thinks money is the most important thing in their life might drive around in an expensive car and feel good, but not everyone even knows how much this car costs. We each invest different things with different meanings.' He paused and cocked his head to one side. 'Do you find this an interesting point? I see you are smiling.'

'You could say that,' I said, and settled back into his deep, comfortable chair.

150

The Morality of Tools

One Monday night in the early autumn, when Anne was away on a business trip and I was spending a week at Rose Farm writing up stories, Guy arrived home from Croskill's an hour earlier than usual, and changed into tidy clothes. At teatime, he was clearly trying to eat his gammon steaks as quickly as he could without drawing a warning about indigestion from Mum.

As he waited for his coffee to cool, picking off the glacé cherry from a cherry bakewell and laying it distastefully at the side of his plate, he said to me, 'I'm off to B&Q. Do you want to come?'

The B&Q superstore is on the road leading into York, just after the roundabout on the bypass. As Guy had enthusiastically informed me several times, it is one of the biggest B&Qs in the country.

'What do you have to get?'

'Somebody at Brawston's's nicked my pliers,' he said. 'And I want to look at grinders.'

That was a relief. Guy's truck can accommodate large amounts of building materials, and one of his 'rides' to B&Q in the summer had involved the lifting and carrying of heavy objects.

'All right.'

'Hurry up, then.'

*   *   *

Muttering the words from Sheryl Crow's 'Can't Cry Anymore', Guy strode directly through the towering, overlit, orangey shelves to the power

151

tools section. He weighed Bosch, De Walt and Black and Decker angle grinders in his hands, and distractedly rolled the on-off switches with his thumb as he read the spec cards.

Feeling boredom creeping in, I enquired as to who stole Guy's pliers.

'This bloke called Simon. He's a twat with tools. He's always after borrowin' stuff.'

'Can't you ask him for them back?'

Guy's tool-loving face assumed an expression of weary exasperation. 'No,' he says. 'I can't. That's like accusing somebody of thieving.'

'But if he's going to borrow them—'

'Yes, but that's why you don't borrow tools in t' first place. They can't say no if you ask, but you forget to give 'em back, and then they can't say owt wi'out making out you'd nicked them. So you just don't ask in t' first place, and you make sure you keep your own and everybody else keeps theirs. It isn't very difficult.'

'It doesn't sound like it.'

'Too difficult for fucking Simon, though,' he said. 'But he's only about seventeen, so he'll learn. Probably when somebody starts nicking his tools.'

'Who would have thought it could be so complicated?'

He glanced up from a green Bosch grinder and shot me a bit of a look.

'It's not complicated, it's simple.' I thought I saw him grin as he said this.

'I was only joking.'

'I'm only saying you should respect a tool regardless of whether it's your own or not. It's rubbish about saying bad workmen blame their tools, you know. Good tools make all the difference.'

As we walked back to the truck, with Guy swinging a new set of pliers by his side, I pointed out that he had spent the same amount of time browsing B&Q's power tools as I had done in book shops on our troublesome joint shopping trips in the past. This, as I now reminded him, had usually prompted him to say he didn't understand anyone spending so long looking at things they did not intend to buy.

'Well, I just love tools.'

'Well, I just love books. I don't see you accepting that as an argument.'

'But tools are more interesting than books.'

'Not necessarily.'

'Yes they are.' He definitely grinned this time. 'What have you ever built with a book?'

'Nothing, but somebody could have. It could be a book of instructions.' I was quite pleased with this point.

'No good without tools.'

'Well, when has a tool ever made you look at something in a different way? A tool can't take you off into a different world, can it?'

He opened the back door and, slinging the bag on to a large heap of ropes, said, 'I don't particularly want to be taken off into a different world. I'd rather build things that people can use.'

We got in.

'You know what I mean,' I say. 'What has a tool ever taught you?'

'What has a tool taught me?' he said. 'To keep my fingers out the way when I'm hammering. A very useful lesson.'

I experienced the familiar feeling of being

engaged in an argument that I could not win, but did not mind. My opponent was happy knowing what he knew, and he knew that he wasn't hurting anyone else by knowing it. I laughed. And then for some reason he looked at me, and he laughed as well. He twisted the key so the rattle of the diesel engine drowned out our laughter, and then gestured at the Walkman on the dashboard, inviting me to whack it. With Sheryl Crow cooing and yee-hawing, we pulled into the late-night traffic on the ring road and aimed up towards the black hills of home.

The Virtual World

My old schoolfriend Billy Hodgson lived in a cosy Edwardian terrace overlooking the livestock market in Winterswick. After he left school he had studied town planning, and then gone to work at the county council headquarters in the handsome, stone-and-brick town twelve miles to the north of Sowthistle. He oversaw developments in the town, villages and the country, and worked on nature-conservation projects with the blend of idealism and practicality you find in people who have committed themselves to working for the public good. We had remained friends since school, and I had watched him take a personal, practical enjoyment of the countryside learned growing up in a village outside Kirksfield, feed it with training, reading and thought, and discipline it into lessons he could apply.

There had never been much that was whimsical

154

or romantic about Billy's interest in protecting badgers or sowing wildflower swards: he just believed in the practical benefits of having good things around you. That included shiny modern things like pop music, well-engineered cars and attractive kitchen appliances, as well as birds and native broad-leaved tree species. Billy taught himself to recognize bird songs by listening to recordings of them on a Technics CD deck, and the sturdy boots and check shirts he wore on site visits were well-polished and ironed. He could seem to be all opposites: fan of rugby league, male voice choirs and real ale as well as a connoisseur of dance music, Italian cooking and interior design; ribald and cynical when he talked about Winterswick, but unironically, unsnobbishly devoted to serving the public good. He was also, in a small Yorkshire market town with its fair share of tight-lipped Tories and Tetley Bittermen, gay— although he had limited interest in the mainstream gay scenes in cities like Leeds and Manchester. Sometimes when Billy came to Rose Farm when we were younger and he had not come out, he would flip through the *Farmer's Weekly* in the living room, casting his eye over the personal columns while I thought he was looking for ecology stories.

In Kirksfield and Winterswick there were always tales about straight lads—minicab drivers, bank clerks, tyre-fitters, you name it—who would sometimes come on to men when they were drunk, saying even as they did that they were not gay, and were just messing about for a laugh. I thought the gossip that gave such stories their circulation might make life hard for Billy, but when I asked him about it, he usually just shrugged. There were a few nudges and sideways looks, and in the next town going north, a gay council officer he knew had been shoved up against a toilet wall and threatened with slander by a local businessman whose planning application had been turned down. But generally, he said, he didn't think it was any worse than it would be in other places, and you just got on with it. The worst thing had been whispering and pointing across a bar from men who had been his friends for years, and that could happen anywhere.

His partner was a Leeds man who had left coal mining to train as a dental technician. They were thinking of going to live in York, he told me one night when I drove up to have a drink with him.

'But won't you miss living here?' I asked him. 'With your job you seem like you're properly part of a community. And they're nice places, all those villages and Winterswick—'

Billy screwed up his face at this. 'I think you're idealizing it all a bit, old chum. There's nothing perfect or uniformly kind about rural communities. There's just a lot of propaganda that says so.'

'But . . .' I told him about going out driving with my brother, but it came out sounding pathetic. 'It's just that when Guy's talking about fields he knows and tracks he's driven down, it's like he's got a link and a purpose that I don't have. I'm not mystifying it, I'm just saying it's maybe something people don't realize they have until they've lost it.'

'But Guy works on the land, for someone who owns it. You don't get many people in modern rural communities with that sort of link with their landscape any more. Most of them have a stronger

156

link to their local town or city.'

'But you have a link with it.'

'Yes, but I have links with urban centres as well. I get my entertainment and shopping in a city. If I went to hospital it would be in a city. The influence of attitudes held in Leeds are felt on people sixty miles away. You can't think of places as being that separate any more.'

A compère switched on a microphone to announce a pop quiz, and a woman came round handing out photocopied answer forms. Billy went to fetch two more pints of bitter and some pickled eggs from the bar. I listened to a DJ playing introductions from old chart hits, and wished I hadn't mentioned the trips with Guy.

'Cheer up, sunshine.' Billy lowered the pints on to the table, and then brought over the eggs, which were in bun cases, and a packet of salt-and-vinegar crisps. The barmaid had suggested that we crumble the crisps, then roll the eggs in the flakes. They tasted good with the beer, and so we got more of both and tried answering the quiz questions. At the end, I tried to say what I had meant earlier.

'The thing is, Billy, when I think about what you do, it makes me realize that I've never really looked at the country around me and thought about it. And I think that if people did just think about the world around them as they walked through it, why it was there, why it looked how it did, whether they were happy with it, then the world would start to become better because we'd think about what we wanted.'

He looked at me with slight bemusement. 'Well, I agree with your basic point.'

157

'And you're looking after those animals and those landscapes . . . I'm just saying it seems inspiring to me, that's all.'

'Well, thanks, but you know—' he said, and took a drink, 'I've changed my mind a bit over the last few years. I used to think planting a few trees or conserving a badger sett was earth-shatteringly important, but now I think you also have to ask if it really makes a difference to people's lives. The fact is that it would make more difference to more people if they had a good sports centre built locally than if they saw a badger. You have to measure the benefits of things. You have to avoid projecting your idealized vision of somewhere on to it, and ignoring the realities of the people in that place.

'Quite a lot will just carry on anyway with a bit of support and protection, because it's got nature behind it. Nature restores, so a lot of it will come back if you look after it a bit. People need a bit more effort, but it's people that really matter. And now I look at cities, and I see authorities making changes and developments that make people really excited. They make cities become vibrant, interesting places. Compared with them what is there to be really *excited* about in modern rural life? The problem is that nice rural areas have not been *made* nice by people. They were nice forty years ago, and we've just kept them that way. That makes people scared of change, but change can be a good thing! It can make people's lives richer—it isn't about taking away all the time.'

*　　　*　　　*

Autumn came, and I stopped going to see the

158

psychoanalyst, after a total of ten visits. It was beginning to get expensive, and he had started asking questions about masturbation for which I did not yet feel ready. Also, rather than getting hooked on the visits, I wanted to think about what I had learned, and to help with this I started a list which read as follows:

1. Youth/Age
When you are young, you feel lost and wrong in ways that you think are unique and special. When you are old you realize that everyone feels lost and wrong. Our characters develop out of the things we do to hide this.

2. Love/Protection
Sometimes when you try to protect someone, you end up making them mistrust everyone in the world except you. Feeling that much mistrust causes the sort of pain you were trying to protect them from in the first place.

3. Happiness
Happiness—is it a) a state of constant joy, b) a general sense of contentment or c) just an absence of unhappiness? Is it different for different people?

The list stopped there, because I stopped to try to figure out the happiness question, and never got beyond it. I wrote it down because the analyst had once asked me when I was last happy, and I hadn't answered the question.

Happy? I felt the sort of flustered vacancy I got when I wanted to leave my house and realized I didn't know where my keys were. It wasn't that I thought I was any less happy than most other people, just that like most other people, I didn't give happiness much thought.

'Um . . . on holiday?'

'I am not looking for the right answer, I am looking for your answer. When would you say you were last happy?'

'Well, on holiday then.'

'And when apart from being on holiday?'

I said I would think about it for our next meeting, but thankfully he did not bring it up.

*   *   *

Also in the autumn, a friend sold me a cheap PC which I gave to Mum and Dad as a present, thinking they would enjoy using the Internet on dark nights. As Dad watched, Mum said, 'I don't know if we'll be able to manage it,' and jumped when she clicked the mouse. But I showed them how to find the Internet, and my mum typed 'Sowthistle' into Google and got a picture of the church, and the next week they signed up to a course with the adult education centre in Kirksfield. Soon they began going online themselves, and trawling historical and local sites. Together they collected information about gardening and birds and legends, stories about the Wild West and the West Riding and the weather. 'It's great, the Internet,' my mum said to me one

160

Friday that autumn when I had just arrived from London. 'I was miles away the other night, with cowboys and Stone-Age people and all sorts. Apparently we're in the virtual world now.'

Unpleasant Pheasant

One Sunday later that autumn, my mum was putting a roast chicken on the table for dinner when Guy arrived back from his morning's work carrying two cock pheasants strung together with baler twine round their necks.

'What the hell have you got in your hand?' asked Helen, who had come to visit.

Guy looked at the birds, and then back at her. 'Two dead pheasants,' he said.

'Jesus Christ, it's like Wuthering bloody Heights! *Why* have you got two dead pheasants? And stop there with them, thank you.'

Guy was holding the birds out towards her.

'I'm only showing you. They're an early Christmas present from a friend of Jim's. He shot them on Highthorpe Estate.'

He jiggled them towards her like puppets, and then hung them by the baler twine on the handle of the kitchen door.

'Can't you put them somewhere else?' said Helen, appalled. 'I'm trying to eat my dinner. There are laws about things like that.'

'I thought you might be interested to have a look. They're pretty.'

'Well, I've seen them now. And they're dead.'

Guy shrugged, unhooked the birds and went

161

outside to hang them with the onions in the outhouse.

'I can't believe he gets that as a present,' said Helen.

'I think it's good,' I said. 'It's better than someone buying you a bottle of whisky or giving you a bonus.'

'That's exactly what someone who lives in a city would think. I hate to remind you, but Guy doesn't like pheasant any more than I do.' She looked at Mum for sympathy. 'Poor things, how could you shoot 'em?'

'They wouldn't be there if someone didn't breed them for shooting,' I said.

'They'd be better off not being born at all if their life serves no other purpose than to be shot,' she said, reaching for the vegetable pasta bake. 'That argument's pathetic.'

'It depends on how you look at it.'

She turned sharply and stared at me. 'What's with you, man-o-' the-country? I suppose you'll be going fox-hunting with your new friends this afternoon?'

'No, but I am going lamping with Kevin soon.'

Helen looked from Mum to Dad to Guy and then back to me. 'Are you joking?'

'No.'

'Freak.'

'Jack Gemble reckons t' lampers are shooting all t' owls,' said my mum. 'And he thinks they got a fox he'd been getting tame. It used to come and eat out of his hand.'

*   *   *

Kevin was the site foreman in the yard. He was in his early thirties, tall, with a sunburned face and an open, talkative nature. A few weeks before that Sunday, the builders' JCB had burst a hydraulic pipe, and he had come to ask my mum and dad if they knew anyone who could repair it. They directed him to Cudlipp's agricultural engineers in Northburn, but then all three got to talking about the Wolds, and Kevin got to talking about hunting. He sometimes followed the fox hunt, but mostly he went shooting—stalking deer, or lamping rabbits, hares and foxes with high-power hand-held lamps that dazzled them. Shooting was his relaxation and his adrenalin fix, and as he talked about the lanes and tracks he used, the animals he saw and the apparent power of moonlight over them, his face grew as animated as that of a children's party entertainer. He began to come up to the house several times a week, and one afternoon when I was there listening to him talking about the moonlight in a particular dale, I said: 'I've never been hunting.'

'Take you out, if you want,' he said, clearly joking.

'I don't think—' said my mum.

'All right,' I said. 'When?'

*   *   *

No one in my family went lamping, or to proper shoots, but my dad did keep an old shotgun, first in the crockery cupboard and then, when the law changed, in a locked metal box in the hallway. Sometimes he would put it in the tractor cab if he was working somewhere where there was a lot of

163

game. When Eileen and Howard came to visit, he and Howard, who also had a shotgun, would sometimes go up the lane and shoot a couple of rabbits, or a pheasant, or a couple of partridges, and bring them back for Mum and Auntie Eileen to pluck, skin, gut and cook for Sunday dinner.

These mornings were later cited by Helen as reasons for her vegetarianism, and she claimed a sort of spiritual kinship with one pheasant that, having been shot and stashed in a tractor cab by my dad, came back to life and flapped around his head until he managed to open the back window and let it out.

'It serves you right,' said Helen when this incident was recounted. 'It was its ghost coming back to haunt you for all the pheasants you and Uncle Howard shot.'

'Tha ate pheasant when tha were little,' he said. 'So it'll be coming back to haunt thee as well then.'

'It didn't mean I liked it. I thought I had to eat it. The pheasant will know I'm its friend, and it'll let me off.'

'What about when me and your dad put hay and barley out for t' pheasants and rabbits in winter?' said Mum. 'He's their friend then.'

'They're not fooled,' said Helen. 'They're just hungry, and it isn't the same thing.'

Our family was even more divided on the subject of fox-hunting. When Helen, Guy and I were teenagers, just passing a hunt on a family car trip was enough to start an argument. Helen and I, who both hated it, complained loudly. Guy didn't commit either way but said it was an excuse for drinking and meeting up, and that he had heard that what people really liked was getting so fired up by the chase that the parties afterwards were wild and ended in lots of sex. Mum said she hated it because she thought it cruel to dig out and let the hounds tear apart the fox. Like many people in Sowthistle, she and my dad never used the plural 'foxes', but always talked about 'the fox'. If my dad saw one late at night on the combine, he would, on getting home, tell us he'd seen the fox that night; when one came and took one of the cats, Mum said the fox had got it. Only when one was spotted run over by the side of the road did they call it *a* fox. It was as if alive, the individual animals were all manifestations of the same creature. It was the same with birds (the blackbird, the wren, the blue tit, though crows and starlings were indefinite). My dad said, 'If they don't hunt 'em, they shoot 'em, and when they shoot 'em half of t' time they miss—and letting one die slowly like that's worse than letting dogs on it'. Sometimes he told a story about a local estate gamekeeper who used to keep two foxes in a cage, so that when a member of the royal family came to stay he could take one, break one of its hind legs, and then set it loose so that the royal family member's party would get a kill.

'That makes me sick,' I would say.

'Well, that's what they do,' he said.

'Don't you think it's wrong?'

'It doesn't matter what I think.'

'It does, though . . .'

At the time I hated that fatalism—people were always telling you that that was just how things were, somehow 'natural' and therefore beyond your control. If someone had power over you it might not be right, but that was just how it was, just like that was how it was when your stock died

165

or the cold made the pipes in the yard freeze. But people did not always obey the laws of nature—anyway, wasn't every waking moment at Rose Farm spent trying to overcome them? It would have been 'natural' to let all the pigs die when a disease came. Surely life was a matter of human intervention as well as of nature?

Anyway, it *did* matter a little bit what he thought. Or rather, what he and my mum thought. In the days when they owned the four fields, they received an annual letter from the head of the local hunt, requesting permission to ride over their land in pursuit of the fox. This prompted an argument which followed the same pattern every year. Dad, sitting at the breakfast table, would slit the envelope with the back of his spoon, see the letterhead, and groan.

Mum, feeding toast crusts to the dog, would look up and ask what he was groaning about.

'It's t' hunt.'

'Well, you know what to do—'

'Mmm.'

'Just write back and tell them they've not to come.'

'I don't know if I can this year—'

'Of course you can. It's a free country and they're your fields, aren't they?'

'I know, but . . . They can make things unpleasant for you if they want, you know. They remember,' he said. 'Maybe we'll just not answer this year, and then they'll come if they want, eh?'

'Fine,' said Mum. 'I'll go and stand in front of t' hedge and tell 'em myself.'

This was how my dad came, every year, to write a letter to the hunt respectfully refusing permission to ride over his four fields.

Since the sale of the land, my dad had used his gun only to shoot at pigeons and crows in his sheds. Locked away in the steel cupboard, it had long ceased to be any sort of family issue. However, in a very different way, it was about to become one again.

The Shotgun

During the summer he had spent working with the straw, my dad had regained much of his old personality. It was as if returning to familiar, instinctive patterns of work and rest somehow eased and revived him. By Christmas he was once again talking to Guy about the weather and the land, and watching the Westerns that my mum taped from the television.

Then one morning in the winter he received a letter from the Humberside Police.

A few months before, he had filled in and sent off, as he usually did, the form for renewing his shotgun licence. There had been a question about medication taken in the last twelve months, and because the last of Dr Wilkinson's prescriptions had fallen within that period, he had ticked the 'yes' box. As the letter explained, because of new laws introduced to reduce gun crime, this meant he had to be interviewed by a doctor before the police could renew his licence. There was a number to call, and he rang to make an appointment at a hospital outside Hull.

The night before the appointment, I sat with my

167

mum and dad in the kitchen as my mum put an old tea towel around his shoulders and cut his hair, scattering black and silver curls over his ears and eyelashes. He sat still, quiet, tapping the back of one hand with the thumb of the other.

'What does tha think they'll ask me?' he asked my mum.

'I think they'll just have a conversation and ask you what you've been doing. When I rang t' doctor he said they'll just sit and have a chat with you.'

'Do you reckon it'll be a feller or a woman?'

'It just says Dr O'Shea. I don't know. It'll not make any difference though, will it?'

'No, no. I was just wondering.'

'I tell you what, lad,' she said in a sort of mock-threatening voice, taking the scissors from his sideburns and waving them at him like an interrogator, 'I reckon we're going to discover all your secrets. I'm going to find out everything you've been hiding from me all this time!'

At this, he smiled a broad, slow, benevolent smile, ripe with relaxed gratitude. 'Oh, aye,' he said, and winked at me. 'Game's up now.'

In the morning he put on his blazer, a tie, a pair of grey trousers and his best brown shoes. My mum wore a smart blouse and a skirt. They set off for the hospital, leaving far more time than it would take to get there.

In the kitchen after they'd gone I sat on my own for a bit, with just the sound of the clock ticking and the fridge humming. I thought about my dad sitting in an office or surgery with pastel-coloured walls and stacking chairs and a desk. I wondered how he was feeling as he talked to a stranger about being down. I hoped they would let my mum go in

168

with him, and I hoped it was an older doctor.

I thought about a couple of times, now both years ago, when I had asked him about his feelings. Once, when I was about ten, and we were coming in from feeding the pigs on a winter night, I asked him if he would mind if I didn't become a farmer. I had spent the hour it took to feed all the animals wondering about the question. He said no, not if I didn't want to, and when we walked up the path he put his arm around my shoulders.

The other time came about ten years later when I asked him why he loved my mum. I was as uneasy about asking that as I had been about the other question, but he just wrinkled his brow for about five seconds and said, decisively, 'Because she respected me.'

I felt as if I had been told something profound about life but had failed to understand it, and my reply came out sounding ridiculously offhand. 'Oh, right.'

As I sat in the kitchen, I looked out of the window, past some quarrelling blue tits, at the old brick barn, which was now being converted to a house. I thought about nursing the sick pigs in there in the summer holidays, and that brought back another memory. At the beginning of the second-to-last summer before I left home, some of the young weaner pigs became infected by a meningitis virus. At first their heads dropped, and then after a few days their droopy heads swung erratically when they walked, as if they had heavy weights rolling around inside their skulls. After a week, they became unable to stand, and eventually they lay still, hungry and thirsty but unable to get to the water or feed troughs.

169

We took the pigs with the disease out of their pens, and put them in a sort of sickbay in the barn, just under the slits that let in the light. We built a little wall of hay bales, put two small troughs for water and feed inside, and Mum diverted the leftovers from the hens to the sick pigs. Every day at the end of feeding up, I held the pigs to the water trough and pushed their snouts under to make them drink.

Most of them wasted away quickly and died, but one gilt that fell ill at the end of July hung on into the middle of August, and I thought that, with a bit of extra care, I could save her. I called her Sam. Sam seemed to want to drink, but she thrashed about when I held her to the trough, as if she disliked being touched. She got a wild, fearful look in her eye however gentle I was, and she tried to wriggle out of my grasp even when she was at her weakest. In the end I used to sit in the pen with her across my lap, trying to pour water from an old pale-green Tupperware jug into her dry, ridgy mouth. I dissolved feed pellets and mashed potato in water, poured the mixture into her mouth, and held it shut to make her swallow.

One or two pigs had recovered from the illness, and I thought Sam was showing promise. I got my dad to have a look at her. He raised his eyebrows and said, 'Aye, well. Keep trying wi' it.' So I did.

When the combining started and we wolfed sandwiches for tea so that we could get back to work, I left my cups of tea so that I could spend five minutes trying to pour water into what I finally had to admit was a whitening, wasting pig. I had once bought my dad a book called *The Prevention of Pig Disease* from the stationer's-cum-bookshop in Kirksfield as a birthday present. I found it in a bookcase among James Herriot memoirs, Fred Truman biographies and local history books, and looked for tips, but its tables and technical language brought on the same fog as reversing a four-wheel trailer.

Sam's bristles grew thicker and longer, and lice and flies gathered among them. Her eyelids drooped, and her inky blue eyes seemed to be slipping into her skull. One teatime when I tried to feed her, she did not swallow even when I held her snout and mouth together. I held her in my lap and in the dark of the barn, with sun-bars of dust coming through the slits and shining down about us, said out loud, 'Please don't die.'

When I heard Guy's tractor coming into the yard with a load of wheat, I laid Sam on the straw and went to guide him back. We emptied the grain into the pit and I shovelled it up neatly and then I went back to the quiet, dark barn. She was laid flat out and still. I climbed in and slid my palm between her left front legpit and ribs. Her bristly skin was only just warm, and there was no heartbeat. Later on I would have to throw her on the muck-cart and take her up the lane to bury her, but for now I left her where she lay.

When my dad, Karl and Guy came back into the yard that night at about ten, I waited until everything was put away before I said anything.

'That pig died, Dad,' I said, as we were walking up to the house.

'Oh, bloody hell, lad,' he said, in a consoling voice.

'I tried wi' it. I thought it was going to do it, like, but—'

171

'Never mind,' he said. 'You can't do much wi' 'em once they stop eating. They gi'e up theirsens, some of 'em.'

I realized then that he had known all along the pig would die.

The blue tits flew off, and the day ticked on.

* * *

The car door slammed, their voices grew louder as they came up the path, and my mum and dad walked in, beaming and joking.

It was as if they had been to visit long-lost friends and found that they still got on very well. The doctor had been an Irishwoman of about fifty, and from farming stock herself. She'd let Mum come in, and she'd asked my dad to tell her about his life, starting from when he was born. My mum said it had been awkward at first, but once he'd got going there was no stopping him. The doctor had said, 'Well, it sounds like there's no wonder you've been a bit down.' My mum had said, 'He's got quite good at bouncing back', and the doctor agreed, and said it was ridiculous that someone like him had been asked to do something like this, but you had to be so careful—and that was it. 'She was smashing,' said my dad, top button undone, tie loosened and jacket flapping open. I suppose no one had ever asked him to tell the story of his life before.

'I don't think we discovered any secrets, though,' said Mum.

Rats

On a Sunday afternoon the following spring, Guy took me out driving along the narrow roads around one of the northern Wolds' deserted medieval villages. The roads had grass growing down the middle, with groundsel and daisies peppering the green, and the Fourtrak's roof rattled the low overhanging branches of elder trees. When we came to the tops of hills, we could see the coastal plain and the sea glittering on the horizon.

'Could you slow down a bit?' I said. 'I want to take it all in.'

'Fair enough,' Guy said, and braked hard enough to send the contents of the dashboard showering over my knees and the floor.

'That OK?' he asked.

'Yes, thank you.' I began replacing the flotsam from the dash—pens, mobile-phone cover, vacuum flask, inspection record sheets for Jim's granary, notebook for recording the ear-tag numbers of his bullocks. 'Don't lose any of that,' he said, smiling. He seemed to be in a pretty good mood.

'Can I just turn the music down a bit as well?'

'All right, but LET ME DO IT though, thank you,' he said. The Discman was playing Blue Oyster Cult's 'Don't Fear the Reaper'. As we were leaving Sowthistle, Guy had claimed his tastes were becoming more varied. However, he had now had the same song on repeat for twenty-five minutes.

'It's amazing up here, isn't it?' said Guy. 'Look

at that fucking view.'

'Fantastic.'

'You could just do anything up here, couldn't you? No one would ever know. Imagine living there—' he indicated a big farm on the brow of the hill to our right. 'You could work naked all day and no one'd ever see you.'

I considered this statement for a moment. 'Would you *want* to work naked?'

He sighed. 'You know what I mean. And anyway, you might want to work naked in t' summer.'

'I suppose so.'

'HANG ON—'

Suddenly he pulled the steering wheel sharply right. We lurched, and sheets, flask, notebook and pad flew off the dashboard again. Then, shouting something which might have been 'You fucker!', he yanked back left, and I felt myself being flung against the passenger door. Then he was straightening out this sudden kink, with the Fourtrak's back end swinging across the road.

'Don't Fear the Reaper' stalled, and then began playing again. 'What did you do that for?' I said.

'Din't you see? There was a rat ran in front of us.'

'I didn't think you'd swerve to miss a rat.'

'I swerved to *hit* it.'

'Of course.'

'Missed, though.'

'I don't want to be funny, but was it worth bothering?'

He pulled a mildly pained expression. 'Oh, don't start. I fucking hate rats. If you had to work with 'em—'

'I'm not particularly pro-rat myself. I just don't risk tipping my car over for one.'

'I didn't nearly tip it over! If you want to see it nearly tipping over I can do better than that—'

'All right, all right, you didn't nearly tip it over. But I still don't think it was worth the bother.'

'It is when you hate them as much as I do.'

'Well, I think most people would say they hated them. They're vermin.'

'Yeah, but I don't hate them because they're vermin. I hate their character—'

'Guy, are you sure that—?'

'—evil, pure evil. They cause damage for no reason, and they hate you just as much as you hate them. I can't stand them, and they know it.'

'. . . Right.'

'I was cleaning out this corn pit at Jim's one afternoon—it's like this sort of cone shape set into the ground with a big bin all round it, you know— and I'm down in t' bottom of it, sitting on t' sloping bit, and I saw this big fucking rat, nearly as big as a little rabbit, like. I had a shovel handy so I stood up and chucked it blade first, thinking I'd cut it in half. But I fucking missed and slipped down on my arse, and then I'm telling you, no word of a lie, t' rat starts coming up towards me, and it's coming up between my legs like it's going for my bollocks.' He paused as he changed down a gear to take a corner. 'Anyroad, I thought, "You'd better get this right first time", and I waited till it got up between my thighs and then just punched its head.'

I grimaced.

'It wasn't that bad,' he said. 'I was wearing gloves. But I'm telling you, it changes your outlook if you've had a rat after your knackers.'

I smiled, and he chuckled. 'Country ways, bro, country ways.'

Girl in a Land-Rover

My dad and I had gone up to the spinney to feed Double and Trouble, and were talking to Jack Gemble at the gate.

'Gran' neet,' he said.

'Aye,' conceded my dad.

'Reckon we might 'ave some rain though.'

'Aye. It's been dry, an't it?'

'Oh aye, and—who's this?'

An old Land-Rover pulling a small, low trailer crunched up the lane and then, to our surprise, turned into the spinney. A young blonde woman of about thirty was driving, with a chocolate Labrador in the passenger seat.

'Is she summat to do wi' thee?' Gemble asked me.

The woman wore blue Argyll wellingtons and a green padded waistcoat. She had pulled her hair back in a rough ponytail, and the bit of wind blowing across the exposed hillside was pulling strands of it out on to her face. She shoved her fingers as far as they would go into her front jean pockets, leaving her thumbs outside, and greeted us with a Land-Rover-owning breeziness.

'Hello!' she said, looking at my dad. 'Are you Mr Benson?'

'I am, love.'

'Your wife said you might have one or two bales of straw. I'm looking for some small bales and I

176

can't find anybody who does them.'

My dad's baler made old-fashioned small bales of the size you see in television dramas in which characters in rural locations are required to carry straw about. As farms had grown larger, these dimensions had grown outdated: most bales were now about five feet high, and had to be moved with a fork-lift truck.

'Aye,' said my dad, with a somewhat brisker tone than he had been using to discuss the impending rain. 'We'll fetch you some.'

Gemble and I looked at each other blankly, and I followed Dad to the stack. We put half a dozen bales into her trailer, and she gave my dad ten pounds, which was well over the going rate. She said the straw was for her horse: she had just one, in a stable over at Winterswick, and the large bales everybody made now were too big for its needs.

'Will you be doing any more in future, Mr Benson?'

'All being well,' he said.

'Good! Maybe see you again then!' She drove away with the straw bouncing in the trailer behind her. My dad shrugged his shoulders at me.

'Don't get any ideas, she only wants you for your straw,' I said.

'Don't get cheeky, son,' he said, smiling. 'Anyroad, at that price she's bloody welcome to it. Come on, let's go and take this money down to your mother before we spend it.'

*   *   *

The woman in the Land-Rover proved to be the start of something. Shortly after her visit straw

177

merchants from the Lake District and the Yorkshire Dales began telephoning to ask if they could come and buy lorry-loads of small bales. There was a fair market for them, they said, leaning against their trucks, wiping wet foreheads after roping down their loads. All the people moving out of Leeds and Manchester wanted ponies and horses, and all the stables needed straw.

My dad decided that he could handle more if he could load bales on to a trailer without uncoupling the tractor, but that meant he would need another machine to load the bales. He saw in the *Kirksfield Gazette* an advertisement for a farm sale which was to include a second-hand fork-lift, and asked me if I wanted to go with him, just for a look.

The Sambron, which was in good condition, fetched £2,000. I had some money from my redundancy; on the way home in the hire car, I said to my dad maybe I could help him buy a fork-lift if he found one.

'I don't know about that,' he said. 'I think tha should look after thy money.'

'I am looking after it,' I said, which I knew didn't make sense, but I was blathering. Apart from anything else, I felt weird driving with my dad in the passenger seat. 'It might as well do that as sit in a bank, and you can pay me back with your horse-straw fortune.'

He didn't say anything, but raised his eyebrows and nodded his head.

'You can paint my name on it and say "sponsored by".'

'I could if tha liked.'

'I'm joking, Dad.'

'I know,' he said.

*   *   *

Two months later, I was sitting with Mum in the kitchen at Rose Farm when Dad and Guy came in. They had been working at Jim Croskill's, using the fork-lift they had recently bought, second-hand, from Warkup's. Dad asked me to come outside and have a look at it.

The orange, angular four-wheel-drive FDI Sambron 2065 was parked in the garden. It was a modern-looking machine, with a single extending arm—strictly speaking, a teleporter, as my dad explained.

'What's tha think?' he asked.

'It looks all right.'

'It bloody is all right. Let's show thee.'

He clambered into the cab, fired it up and reversed back a bit so there was plenty of room in front. Then he pushed a lever which made the hydraulic arm, with its two forks, extend slowly up until it was as high as the roof of the house.

'You'll shift some straw with that,' I shouted over the noise of the engine.

'Not half. Do you want a sit in it?'

He got out, and I got in, and under instruction I pulled in and extended the arm, into and out of the pale-blue sky. Then I turned the machine off and got out, and walked around it, looking. Standing where my dad couldn't see, I wrote my name with my index finger in the oily dirt on the engine cover.

When he came around my side of the fork-lift, my dad saw me writing. 'What's tha doing?' he said

179

cheerfully, and I immediately realized how ridiculous this situation was. I rubbed my name off very quickly. 'Nothing!' I said. 'Are we off back inside then?'

The Roebuck

Kevin took me hunting one night the following autumn. I drove to his semi-detached house in Kirksfield as darkness was falling. First he took me into the garden shed where he was sorting ammo with his friend Pete, a plasterer in his mid forties with a brush moustache and an unblinking stare. Pete was friendly, but obviously a man of few words. He wiped the gunpowder off his right hand to shake mine, said, 'Now then, pleased to meet you,' and went back to packing bullets into casings on the workbench, which was covered with bullet presses, powder measures, beam scales, tools and jars of American-import gunpowders. The shed, and Kevin and Pete, smelled of stale fireworks and mud.

Kevin told Bess, his black Labrador, to stop licking my fingers, and talked me through the rifles and full-metal-jacket bullets, lead-shot cartridges, and V-maxes with red plastic tips that exploded on impact. 'Give summat a hell of a knock,' he said.

He went into the house to tell his wife Lynne that we were leaving. I asked Pete what his and Kevin's wives thought of hunting, and he said they didn't mind, but they didn't really understand it either. 'I remember once, I had my sights on this deer. We'd driven out into some fields straight

180

from work, and it were quiet as owt—lovely. I was just getting him in my crosshairs, waiting for him to come up from this bit of scrub, and suddenly, "Rrring!" Bloody mobile starts going off. So I answer it, and it's Angie, my wife, like. She says, "Hiya, what you up to?" I say, "I'm just trying to shoot a deer, love," and she says, "Oh, right, well I won't keep you—I was just calling to tell you it's frosty, so be careful on t' roads." Bloody deer was off like a shot. Thing is, I would've known it was frosty, cos I'd just been driving, hadn't I? I didn't say owt, though. Just "Thanks, dear."'

'Dear,' I said, with a laugh.

'Yeah.'

'I mean like as in "dear" and "deer".'

Pete moved his eyebrows up a little and said, 'You're not anti-blood are you?'

'No, no, not at all! Not much bothered either way.'

'Right,' he said, and moved his eyebrows down again.

We loaded four rifles, a refrigeration box, high-power field glasses and a 1 million candle-power lamp into Kevin's Fourtrak, and Kevin and Pete put on camouflage jackets. Pete rolled a cigarette and then drove us out along some B-roads. We passed a quarry, a lorry park and a brown sign pointing the way to an Open Farm.

'Hope you're not squeamish,' said Kevin from the front passenger seat.

I thought of watching my mum and dad butchering pigs on the kitchen table. 'No, OK on that score!' I said confidently.

'Right!' he replied. 'Well, what we're going to be doing tonight is looking for some rabbits, for my

181

mate who keeps hawks. On one farm the farmer himself likes us to shoot foxes because they come and take his chickens, but we have to tread a very fine line. This land belongs to Gerald Thwaites, and because he's master of the hunt he wants all foxes to be left, so he can hunt them. It's him who gets me on the land, so I have to tell him I'm not shooting foxes. But if I go and the fox gets a hen that night, the farmer'll get arsey with me and complain to Gerald.'

'But Gerald doesn't want you to shoot foxes.'

'He won't mention the fox, he'll complain about summat else. He'll say I've been driving across his drilling or summat.'

'Or we've missed a rabbit and shot a cow!' said Pete through the fag smoke.

I laughed. 'It's no joke,' said Kevin. 'It happens. People don't always check what's behind where they're shooting. Worst mistake you can make. If you hit a cow, there's hell on.'

'Worst thing is dog walkers,' said Pete.

I looked at Pete's face in the mirror to see if he was joking. Unfortunately it was obscured by his camouflage cap.

'If dog walkers see you shoot owt, especially a deer, they get real upset.'

'Oh, right.'

'Gerald always says, if you see anybody walking a dog, don't shoot. There's been times when I've had a deer right there, you know, but you just can't. It wouldn't be very good PR.'

'It sounds like you wouldn't want to be upsetting Gerald Thwaites,' I said. Pete turned off the main road on to single-track lanes, and then into hilly stubble fields.

182

'No. Like with the hunting: I personally don't agree with fox-hunting, but I have to watch what I say cos he's a very powerful bloke. He's got a lot of money and he's very well respected.'

'Sometimes Gerald Thwaites seems like a mafia don or something,' I said. 'Do you know what I mean?'

'Not really,' said Pete.

'He's very good with me,' said Kevin. 'I'm just some bloke who shoots for him, but when I see him in his office he always gets up from the computer and says, "Hello Kevin".'

*   *   *

We were looking for a roebuck Kevin had seen a couple of times when he was last out stalking. The buck had a broken front leg, and had to lie down to eat. Its herd had abandoned it, and it lived alone on the edge of some woodland.

'You can't shoot deer under a lamp,' said Kevin. 'It's no sport cos they just sort of get hypnotized by the lights. It's illegal, unless it's a humane kill. This is humane because it's swinging—I mean it's swinging its leg, see? It can't feed itself, and its leg's all deformed. It'd starve to death anyway eventually. In the days when deer had natural predators like wolves it'd have been picked off, but now deer's only natural predator is man. That's why you get so many.'

We turned into a field with woods and dales on either side, and in the distance the orange lights of a bypass. There was a full moon, greenish-white as an onion, and the sky was clear. The fields and lanes looked as if they were made of mercury and

183

soot. Pete stopped the Fourtrak and leaned back to heave the lamp, which was like a large black saucepan with a bulb, out from the back seat.

'I thought you were helping,' he said to me.

'Sorry,' I said, and started rearranging the guns.

He plugged the lamp into the cigarette lighter, poked it out of the window and strafed the field. A badger, caught in the light, looked up and ran to hide in bales piled up on the headland. Rabbits scampered into the hedge. Jack Gemble said rabbits and birds were jumpy when there was a full moon.

'Them's deer over there,' said Pete.

In the woods on the far side of the field six green spots, in pairs, were fixed under the lamp. They couldn't turn away from the light, and they couldn't see past it.

Kevin jerked his rifle to his shoulder and squinted through the telescopic sights.

'I don't think that's him,' he said, and rested the gun on the truck door. 'I'm not going to risk it unless I'm one hundred per cent certain it's the swinging one.'

Pete moved us off down tracks into another field, this one lower. We crossed deep tramlines that tossed the Fourtrak about and ruined my rifle arrangement. He scanned the land again. Feeling a rush of excitement, I pointed out something lurking in the hedge bottom.

'What's that, look?' I asked, and pointed over Pete's shoulder through the windscreen.

'It's a bale of straw,' he said.

'Sorry.'

'We put it there because it's where the wind comes down. It stops us getting upwind of them.

Now, that—' The beam rolled over two new green spots.

'That's him,' said Kevin.

Pete pulled up. Kevin got out and rested the rifle barrel on top of the door. The shot was louder than I expected, and immediately after it I felt a pain in my temples from the pressure waves. Inside the Daihatsu there was a sulphurous smell that blew out as Pete drove us over to the deer, with Kevin standing upright on the door ledge.

The roebuck lay as it had fallen in the grass. There was a pencil-width bullet wound in its shoulder, and bubbling black-red lung-blood coming foaming out of its mouth into the soil. The blood steamed in the hunching-cold starlight. In the animal's big, lifeless eye the moon reflected like a tiny star in an empty, dark-blue universe. Pete and Kevin looked at the leg, which was broken in two places, and at the shoulder blade and the hoof, which was warped, one half twice the length of the other. Pete said, 'Poor little bugger,' and Kevin pulled a Sony Sureshot digital camera from his jacket breast pocket, and tried to find the night setting. I put my hand on the roebuck's belly and felt warm blood on my fingers. When I tried to wipe it off, it smelled ferric and became sticky.

'Do you mind if I have a look at that leg?' said Pete. 'Just out of morbid curiosity?'

'Go for it,' said Kevin. 'I want to see if I can get this damn camera to work.' He took three pictures of the roebuck, and then called a friend on his mobile phone, and said something about a V-max in the shoulder knocking the roebuck back five yards.

Pete tugged open his hunting knife and made

185

three light, deft cuts into the skin around the leg. He tore back the skin and then cut away muscle to find the bone. Fresh steam rose into the night air. 'Broken and set, look,' he said, digging into the shoulder and lifting a bone that was all knotty and wrong-angled. 'Even the shoulder's chivelled up. It'll have been hit by a car.'

From between two lumps of purple muscle, Pete's nicotined fingers pulled out a round, fatty, two-pence-sized gland. He trimmed the fat tissue from it so it came loose in his hand. The roebuck's muscles around its belly twitched and spasmed, and my stomach joined in.

'One of his lymph glands,' Pete said, seeing me looking, and holding it up. 'Shouldn't be half as big as that, but there's infection in it.'

'Mmmm.'

'Are you all right?' he said.

I nodded.

Pete gently snorted and smiled, and then sliced the gland. He looked inside and then tossed it into the hedge, and wiped his knife on his jeans.

We set off again, and in another field, so high up we could see the lighthouse winking at Flamborough Head, where the chalk Wolds end at the North Sea, Pete's light caught two yellow eyes staring back at him.

'Fox,' said Kevin. 'I've seen him before. He goes and takes a chicken from t' yard and then comes out here to eat it.'

'Are you going to shoot it?' I did not want to see a dead fox.

'If we can. If there's chicken feathers in this field tomorrow morning, farmer'll be mad with us. We'll see if we can suck him in.'

186

Kevin and Pete put their two hands to their mouths as in prayer, then smacked and sucked their lips together.

'They think it's the sound of a rabbit in trouble,' said Kevin. 'If they're looking for something to eat they come running right up to you.'

Pete eased the Daihatsu forward ten yards, and they got out. Kevin took the lamp, and Pete took his repeat rifle. They walked forward, Kevin shining the light. The orange eyes appeared in the darkness—then disappeared again.

'He's sly,' said Kevin. 'And he could be lamp-shy. If a fox gets shot at under a lamp and escapes, you never get him. He knows what's up.'

We continued like this for some time: advancing slowly on the fox eyes in the dark, Pete getting them in his sights, and the fox retiring further back into the blackness. To the sides of us, deer came and went, and scuttling badgers nipped in and out of the lights.

Eventually the eyes disappeared. The fox blinked himself away into the night, and Kevin and Pete turned their attention to rabbits. They got two, Pete finishing off the last, still-twitching one with a swift, matter-of-fact chop to the back of its neck. Then they unloaded the rifles and passed them to me to stow in the back, and Pete steered the truck back down the rolling tracks to the road. Kevin asked me if I had enjoyed myself, and I said yes. I kept to myself my pleasure in discovering a fox could so easily outwit two men with all their technology, although, as we rattled along in the rutted lanes, I realized that that might be the whole point.

Bulls

My family had settled into its new routines now, but all around us life on the Wolds was changing. The changes were not all about loss: many of them were welcomed by lots of people, and brought new money, work and choices into the towns and villages. Many of them brought replacements for services and goods that were no longer available. Others simply represented the exchanging of one way of life for another.

So, the post offices in every village around Sowthistle were closed, but the county council built small brick huts containing Internet-connected PCs beside ponds and bus shelters. Some businesses in Kirksfield relocated to towns nearer to the M62, but hundreds of new houses were built on the edge of town and in the surrounding villages. Sowthistle got a new brick-built village hall to replace its old wooden one, but when Art Towse retired from winding the church clock daily after thirty years, no one volunteered to replace him.

More small livestock markets closed, but Kirksfield's farmers' market thrived, and more and more farmers and producers began branding their produce and retailing it in farm shops. Up on the high Wolds, two barley growers built a microbrewery and began making their own beer. There were also, on the farms, anxieties about new diseases, new legislation, and new economics that meant that some arable men found it advantageous to sell their tackle and outsource

188

most of the work to contractors. Foot-and-mouth reached the far edge of Jim Croskill's fields. Guy learned how to operate the new centralized, computerized system of passports for cattle and to do the paperwork for the Farm Assured stored-grain monitoring system.

And sometimes, on the farms, there were more sad stories about people that, in the words commonly used by counsellors speaking about the subject on television, made you wonder how amid all that beautiful scenery there could ever be such unhappiness and solitude.

*   *   *

At nine o'clock on a damp Monday morning in March, my mum and I drove silently through the fields and woods to the north of Sowthistle towards Highthorpe. The verge-edges were torn ragged by tractor tyres, extra-wide at this time of year to stop them sinking in the mud, but there was no one out on the land yet. In the woods along the dale bottoms there were snowdrops.

The small gravel lay-by at the edge of the village was packed with cars, and as we entered Highthorpe there seemed to be hundreds more, crowded along the roadside, crammed into farmyards, and parked tight together in the pub car park.

By the gate on the path leading off the main street a middle-aged man in a black frock coat silently directed people down to St Mary's church, which sits in trees down on a dale side.

My mum said, 'When I think of me and your dad coming to pick you up from places, you'd both pile into t' back laughing and joking. I would never have thought this. Look at all these cars. If he could come back now and see all these people . . . and yet when he died he must have felt so alone.'

Stuart Hopkinson, my friend from Kirksfield School, had committed suicide the week before, hanging himself in a barn on Sunday evening after feeding the cows. Billy had rung to tell me. He had said that you heard of a lot of farm lads getting down like that at the moment. No one really knew what had pushed him to it, but there were stories about problems on the farm, a tractor accident, an inexplicable falling-quiet. I knew Stuart had many friends, but I found myself wondering if he had worked long hours on his own and, if he had, what he had thought about. *You get very philosophical out ploughing on your own all day, you know. You always know how it's going to end.*

Mum parked the car at the other end of the village and we walked to the pub car park where we met Billy and two other old school friends. Over the cawing of rooks and crows we could hear the distant gear-changing of feed lorries on the main road to Scarborough, and the footsteps of people walking slowly and self-consciously towards the church. Life seemed slowed down by a shared, unspoken thought: 'This can't really be happening, can it?'

The church was full, and already a hundred-odd people were gathered outside around the door, next to which hung two loudspeakers. Beyond the churchyard and its trees, the treeless dale bottom was silent, windless and empty, the stock not yet turned out for the summer. The churchyard was

190

spotted with dead beech leaves. People clasped their hands in front of them: rugby players, with brows and chins marked by dull red grazes from Saturday's match; farm men with fleeces and work boots under their dark overcoats; auctioneers in brogues and green jackets; bulky farmers buttoned into woollen suits, peering from underneath deep brows and badgery grey hair; dark-suited men and women in their thirties with hair blown about by the wind; valuers, agricultural secretaries, feed and machinery reps. Jim Croskill, Bill Warburton the auctioneer, Mike Skelfe.

By the time the service began there were about three hundred people in the churchyard, and when we sang the last hymn, 'All things bright and beautiful,/All creatures great and small', the men's singing swelled up slowly, deep and low beneath the women's trebles, and the voices seemed to carry out of the churchyard and roll down to fill the dale. I imagined the sweet, low singing flowing down into the more distant dales where Stuart had lived and worked.

Lord of all eagerness, Lord of all faith,
Whose strong hands were skilled at the plane
    and the lathe,
Be there at our labours, and give us, we pray,
Your strength in our hearts—

Women pulled tissues out of pockets and sleeves. Men sniffed hard and looked down.

Stuart's brothers read Psalm 109 and a passage from Thessalonians. A friend spoke and made jokes, defying with humour the idea of a lonely suicide carried out one teatime, after feeding the

191

cattle, in a barn. He said, 'I don't know why you did it but I understand; I don't forgive you but I will never forget you.'

Another friend spoke for longer and seemed about to overflow with tears. In a strong East Riding accent, trying to control his breathing, he said Stuart had an emotional code, and when the last digit clicked into place there was nothing anyone could do about it. Then he asked us to imagine Stuart gone to a better place, walking through a stubble field freshly cut towards the end of summer, his mum on one side and his wife on the other, the children and the dogs running along in front of them. At the end of the field they come to a shed with some just-finished bulls glistening in the sunshine, with no more work to be done, so that he can just stop and look at the bulls, and be content in the field with the people he loves.

The people in church broke into applause when he finished, and there was a feeling of something released.

The family came out and sat in the cars that would bear them off to the East Yorkshire Crematorium. My mum and I hung back to let the crush die down. I looked down into the dale as the churchyard slowly fell quiet. In the flat bottom of it, a man now walked slowly across the fields, alone.

Poetry

After the funeral, I thought about Stuart's friend's description of a heaven where Stuart walked among bulls glistening in the sunshine. It made me think about Mrs Hirst's belief that poetry was something most of us had to rely on others to produce, and thinking about that reminded me of something that happened when I first moved to London.

In my first term at university, Seamus Heaney came to do a reading. I went on my own. He looked older than I had expected, and I found the reading boring, but at the end when everyone crowded around his desk to get their books signed, I joined the queue. When I reached Heaney, he absent-mindedly took the *Selected Poems* from my hand and carried on talking about dinner with a man in a bow tie who had introduced him to the audience. When he passed it back, signed, he looked up at me with a blank smile and I said: 'Mr Heaney, can I ask you something?'

'Eh—OK,' he said distractedly. Quickly turning aside to the man in the bow tie, he said '—about half past eight?'

I started again, garbling: 'You know how in your first books you wrote about the difficult feelings you had about writing and your dad? Well, it seemed like you felt a conflict, but you never seem to resolve it, and I wondered, how did you get past it?'

'Oh,' he said without interest, 'I didn't.'

I stood looking at him, blinking.

'You just realize that life isn't about one thing or the other.'

I stood there waiting for him to say something else, but he nonchalantly turned away from me and took the next person's book to sign. I walked away feeling half let down and half amused.

The thing was, Seamus Heaney was right, and Mrs Hirst had been wrong about poets. How could you say that one person felt more than another? The men at the funeral had always felt the sort of love that makes you see bulls glisten: they just chose to express it only on occasions when it really mattered. Just because you talked about your feelings all the time didn't mean you were any more sensitive, or that you cared more. That was just an idea perpetuated by the modern world, although it had taken me until now to properly understand it.

On the Telly at Last

Almost three years after the sale, the first bungalows on the yard were complete. In what had been the garden at Rose Farm there were now piles of scaffolding for the builders replacing the roof of the barn, and in the old foldyard there was a half-built four-bedroom house. The sour scent of mortar hung in the air, and all around Sowthistle cement mixers rumbled on relentlessly.

There was talk of a national rise in house prices reaching Kirksfield and the villages. Most of the new houses in Sowthistle were bought by professional couples from York, Hull or Leeds,

194

and people said that the young locals couldn't get a look-in. The planning authority made it relatively easy to build on former farms, because their smells and noise went down badly with people moving into new, expensive homes for peace and quiet. Professional couples from York and Hull and Leeds were not backward in exercising their legal rights.

The house-price phenomenon had brought another change for Mal to get to grips with. Eileen had taken a job, driving a delivery van for a vast intensive pig unit out towards Kirksfield. The unit was owned by a company which had been founded by a local farmer in the 1950s, and which now owned seven large pig farms, 9,000 acres of arable land and a pig genetics development company. ('Mal doesn't know what to do with himself,' Mum had explained to me. 'She's got her own van and all sorts.') With the extra money, Eileen had set her sights on a new and more ambitious project: tourism. Next door to the yard Mal rented from the council was a half-acre patch of land that he owned. On that land stood a couple of brick sheds, some grain bins, and a small derelict house in which he stored tools and machinery. Eileen was talking about doing up the house as a holiday home.

Mal discussed this with my mum as he stood on the doorstep of Rose Farm, holding a bunch of chrysanthemums he had brought her from his garden.

'You want to get on wi' it,' my mum said. 'You'll make more out of holidays than you do at farming.'

'Will I?' said Mal. 'I don't see who'd want to

come on holiday to Sowthistle.'

'They wouldn't come on holiday to Sowthistle, Mal! They'd use it as a sort of base.'

'How do you mean, a base?'

'They'd go off travelling round, or go on walks around Highthorpe or Millingholme or out for day trips to t' Humber Bridge or something like that.'

I could tell, even just listening from the kitchen, that from the way she ended weakly on the Humber Bridge, she knew that she had chosen a bad example.

'Why would they want to go and look at a bridge?'

'Because it's *famous*. It's the biggest suspension bridge in the world. Or second biggest, maybe, I don't know. The point is there's all sorts of places. When me and Gordon went to t' Lakes we didn't sit in t' cottage all day. We'd go out in a morning and come back when it was time to go to bed!'

'Well that's t' Lakes. Who'd want to look at it round here?'

'Well, I would. I'll tell you something, Mal, this is a beautiful place if you open your eyes and look, and this past thirty years there hasn't been a single day that I haven't felt privileged to live here, and I should say Gordon's t' same, although we don't say anything about it. There's plenty of folks'd want to come here and I'd be proud to have 'em, so now then.'

Mal nodded slowly, taking this in. 'I shall have to have a think, lass,' he said.

'Yes Mal, we all will. We shall have to . . . get with it!'

There was another small silence. The cement mixer rumbled, and up on the main road two

196

motorbikes screamed past.

Deep in Mal's beard, his tongue clicked against his teeth. 'Get with it,' he said.

*   *   *

Two months later my mum came home from Kirksfield and said she had seen Bill Warburton, the auctioneer, there. 'I said to him it seemed funny living with t' houses where t' yard used to be, and he said with the way house prices are going up we should try to sell t' house. He says people like old farmhouses, and I told him we had damp and a few rotten beams but he said don't bother about that, a lot of people want to come and do 'em up.'

My dad raised his eyebrows.

'But he says we should get on wi' it if we're going to do it because you don't know if t' prices'll go down.'

'I don't know where we'd go,' he said. 'But I don't like living here with those houses there and them in Bob's yard.'

'Bill said it'd be cheapest to build in t' spinney.'

When I visited a month later, Helen came over on Sunday and after dinner Mum told us to come and look at something on the Internet. She wouldn't tell us what it was going to be. Reading from a piece of paper, she typed in a URL for Bill Warburton's website.

'Mum, this isn't another local history site, is it?' said Helen.

'Shut up and watch!'

Slowly, a picture fed down on to the screen. As we saw the roof and then the upstairs windows, Helen, Guy and I went quiet. It was a picture of

197

our house.

My mum turned around and beamed at us. 'There we are, kids,' she said. 'On the telly at last!'

Three Hundred Tons of Grief

On a grass verge along the Kirksfield road, I noticed a bright yellow sign bearing an Asda logo and the words, in type meant to look like chummy handwriting: 'Grown for Asda—bursting with freshness!'

When I got home, Guy was in the sitting room eating his tea and waiting for *The Simpsons* to come on. I asked him if he'd seen the sign. I think he knew that I expected him to be annoyed by it.

'Yeah, there's a Tesco one on t' way to Northburn as well,' he said, offhandedly. 'I think they're good.'

'I thought you'd think it was bad.'

He thumbed through the TV channels. 'Not really. People don't know what's in fields. It's got to be good if they realize what they eat comes out of t' ground and not a packet.'

'What've you been doing today?' I asked him, to change the subject.

'I finished tipping all Jim Croskill's taties into a chalk pit,' he said. 'Been going backwards and forwards all day, done three hundred ton.'

'I bet that pleased him,' I said, thinking this was a joke.

'Should do—he told me to do it.'

'What are you on about?'

'He couldn't sell 'em, and he needed space in

his shed. He couldn't even get anybody to fetch 'em for nowt. He only grows forty-five acre, and t' merchant said they want hundreds of tons a week.' He looked at me for the first time, and adopted a sort of yuppie voice. 'They want a constant uniform supply because that's what supermarkets are asking for. Apparently, as people get into cooking more, they demand constant uniform ingredients.' He dropped the yuppie voice. 'Merchants all want to be selling to food companies and supermarkets, and they want t' same taties all year round, so t' merchants can't be bothering with you if you've only three hundred and fifty tons. So we tip them away for nowt to make room. Three hundred tons of fucking grief.'

'But that's terrible, Guy.'

He shrugged disparagingly. 'Yeah, well. It was terrible, but if you have to get rid of 'em, then you get rid of 'em. We just get on with it, Richard; if they don't sell, they've got to go. You want to be getting back on to t' land, get things tidied up, get that dale sprayed off and grub up some of them hedges.'

Guy grinned his gallows grin again, which meant that he was admitting doing his *Power Farming* thing to annoy me. As Guy and I had talked about farming and food since the sale, he had developed certain recognizable routines. This was the one he followed when he was angry about something, jokingly taking it out on me by adopting an exaggeratedly hard-nosed, eco-unfriendly approach that he knew would annoy me. I had become confused about the arguments, and was now about to pick the wrong time to launch an eco-friendly counter-attack.

199

'Don't say that. I hate it when you come out with all that stuff.'

He gave a short, sharp sigh with which he managed to express multiple tones of derision while also curling up the left corner of his top lip, and said, 'All what stuff?'

'All that ruthless businessman thing. Can I ask you a question?'

'Like, "Why don't you go and find another job?" '

'That's not what I was going to ask, but go on then. Why don't you?'

'Because I don't know what else I'd do.'

In this mood Guy seemed to take delight in finding negative answers to my questions. It drove me insane.

'I think you don't value what you do enough sometimes, you know,' I said. This made his top lip start curling again.

'Oh aye? What's that, then?'

'Making stuff, and growing food. It's a good thing to do, isn't it?'

'I think you'll find it's actually a business, and if you did it you'd find you have to be quite "ruthless", as you call it, to compete.'

'Well it's farmers who come out with all that "guardians of the countryside" thing—'

'*I* don't fucking come out wi' it! And as for growing food, I'd be a lot more popular with most people if we grew dope rather than taties.'

'Whatever,' I said. 'So much for loving your way of life.' I didn't mean this to sound as personal as it did.

'FUCK my way of life, Richard! You just want me here keeping it all nice and green like it was in

200

t' old days, so that when you come to visit in summer it looks all pretty and nice and you can buy your lovely free-range pork and then fuck off again. But why does it have to go back or stay t' same? You like to think *you're* making progress, so why can't I?'

'I'm not saying I don't want it to change—'

'Yeah, but you'd rather it didn't. You're like everybody else. I can't understand why people are so scared of things changing.' He paused. 'I can't understand how Mum and Dad's generation—' he had stopped dealing directly with me now '—can *not* like change when you think about what they've seen in their lifetimes. Think about it, right: our mum and dad saw horses replaced by tractors. They saw cars, planes, computers, plastic, television, radio, mobile phones, music centres, National Health, heart surgery, hip replacements —loads of stuff—all come into day-to-day use. Those things have only made life better, but people still think change is bad. So like wi' food, t' one basic thing you need to function, and another thing that's completely changed, they don't change their attitude. They still think about ration books! But it isn't ration books it's Argos catalogues now, isn't it? Choosing from more stuff than you can imagine, pointing, paying and fucking off with it in five minutes. Our mum and dad have seen more big changes than me and you will ever see.'

He seemed to have talked himself out into some calmer pasture now, so I tried to explain what I meant.

'I don't know, Guy. I just think it was . . . just better when you had small units and a lot of things on every unit so you could feed potatoes you didn't

201

want to your pigs and put pig shit on a muck-hill like we did and then spread it back on your land to grow more crops instead of just using fertilizers.'

He looked at me.

'I just think that, like, our old muck-hill stood for something good.'

'The muck-hill?'

'Yes!'

'Well, you'll be sad to learn you have to be very careful with muck-hills now,' he said. 'They leach into t' soil and poison t' water supply. You have to have a proper run-off and everything.'

'Oh,' I said, and tried to laugh.

'It isn't that simple,' he said. 'There's regulations and paperwork for fucking everything now, cos of all t' food scares. I spent half of yesterday arguing with someone at DEFRA at Northallerton about a bullock number tag. They said it didn't exist on their computer, and I was standing wi' it in front of me—'

'Well, so there should be regulations if it makes people trust the food more—'

'You can say that, but how do people know it's safer? Supermarkets don't tell 'em.'

'Well, you lot should publicize it then, that's what other businesses do. I don't know why you don't do proper marketing. I know loads of people in London who'd love to come up here and see how food's produced. They could go to the Kirksfield Show and all that.'

'Oh, *thank* you,' he said. 'It might come as a shock to you, but I don't think Kirksfield Show's put on wi' t' intention of attracting visitors from fucking London.' Guy began to look pained and angry. He didn't want to be talking about this, but

202

nor could he let it drop. 'It isn't just a matter of good people and bad people is it? How do you draw a line between 'em? It doesn't work like that in real life. You have to think fresh, and that's what I mean about people who've seen all this change, but think old-fashioned. That's your trouble, you want it all to be like, good nice little people here, and baddies there—you always did—but t' world in't like that. You look at life like a . . . fucking kid! You don't just leave it alone and it comes up perfect, it comes in one big bastard mess and tha's to sort it out.'

Maybe it was the thing about being like a kid, maybe it was frustration, maybe it was something else, but for some reason suddenly I felt myself losing my temper. 'I know what the world's like, thank you very much, and I know that if you don't tell people what you've got they don't know it. You should market what you make and compete like everybody else has to.'

He looked at me as he might have looked at a stranger. Then he said, 'When everybody else does it, it isn't usually t' people who make t' stuff that do t' marketing. I do things, I don't talk about them. That's your department, in't it?'

I waited for him to turn and grin, but he didn't. 'You should talk about 'em, then,' I shouted back. 'You should talk to Jim and get him to do something,' I said.

'I'm too busy working, Richard—tipping taties down fucking pits.' He started out of the chair, snatched up his plate and fork, and banged out of the room. After a few seconds I heard the front door slam, and my mum's voice calling after him.

203

A Tender Symphony

After my argument with Guy, I stayed away from
Sowthistle for a few months, and spent all the
summer in London with Anne. On the phone
Mum told me about the people who came to view
the house—there were plenty of them, she said,
some local, many from the south, one couple with
ideas about turning the scullery into an office.
At the end of the summer a couple from
Northamptonshire called Martin bought it. Mrs
Martin was a teacher, and Mr Martin an ex-
venture capitalist who had done well out of the
Internet boom. The money from the sale meant
Mum and Dad could now start work on their new
house in the spinney. I had assumed that while it
was being built they would rent a cottage to live
in, but as Helen told me when I rang her in
September, they had different plans.

'They've bought two static caravans,' she said.
'And a shipping container.'

'A shipping container?'

'I mean, I don't mind the idea of the house,' she
continued, 'but caravans, in a spinney, in winter? I
can't wait for Christmas dinner.'

'But what are they going to do with the shipping
container?'

'What else but keep the furniture in it? Not the
cooker and washing machine, mind you—they're
going in the wooden hut from the garden, which is
going to be the kitchen.'

'And what about toilets?'

'They're putting a cesspit in, but I don't want to

talk about it, thank you.'

I thought about Christmas. I had been thinking of inviting Anne to visit. 'It's going to be very cold,' I said.

'Oh no, not at all. Because, you see, there's going to be a wall of straw bales to block the wind, so it'll be, in the words of our mother, "warm". She says it'll be "an adventure", and I have "no sense of fun".'

'Maybe it will be a bit of an adventure,' I offered lamely.

'Don't *you* start. I'm looking for cottages to rent for Christmas tonight,' she replied. 'Let me know if you want a bedroom.'

*   *   *

One October morning a few weeks later I went back to Sowthistle to help with the moving. When I arrived, the move was well under way. The fork-lift was parked by the side of the road and Major Twist and Guy were carrying plant pots from the garden and stacking them in the fork-lift's bucket. In the middle of the garden stood my dad's tractor. It was backed up to the house so that the rear of a trailer it was towing reached almost to the door. Every few minutes Mum or Dad appeared at the door with a piece of furniture and passed it to Kevin, who then carried it over to the trailer and roped it down.

Inside, Helen was sorting through drawers, packing boxes, and complaining about her parents' reluctance to throw anything away.

'Manuals!' she wailed. 'This family is obsessed by manuals! Every bag of photographs I find has got machinery manuals in it, and they're all ancient—*please* can I throw them away?'

'They might be worth something, those,' replied my mum. 'People collect things like that.'

'Mother, plough manuals from the 1970s are *not* worth anything! I'll buy them off you myself if I can throw them away—'

'Ask your dad. Can you fetch these horseshoes please?'

Helen slung the manuals into a half-full cardboard box and stomped over to the cellar stairs where my mum had found three horseshoes that she and Dad had brought with them from Marwood.

'Aren't they the wrong way up?' said Helen. 'I thought they were supposed to curve upwards. Downwards is bad luck.'

'I think you might be right,' replied my mum. 'Maybe we should leave them till last anyway—'

'Give. Me. The. Horsehoes—oh, hello, Richard. I've got some stuff for you to sort out.'

Helen had found boxes of my old school exercise books, and together we went through them, remembering our Eighties education: Schools Council Project history, slide rules, O-levels and 16-plus. Flipping through my English workbook from my second year, she stopped and laughed. 'Check this out,' she said, ' "The Farmer":

The bulky tank of the farmer
Strides like a giant over the fresh chocolate
    furrows,
His vice fists close around the handles of
    the buckets,
Then the crane-like arms hoist up the loads—

'What was it, the Kirksfield metaphor-using championship?'

'Jesus, Helen.' I tried to snatch the book from her, but she pulled it away and read a bit more.

'The pellets fall into the trough
Like a brown waterfall, cascading into a silver
   river,
As the squealing of the pigs
Reach his ear like a tender symphony—

'*A tender symphony?* That's great, Rich. I often used to think how "tender" the sound of pigs squealing was.'

'I must've thought it sounded nice. Please give me the book back.'

She handed it over. 'It's usually easier to say what sounds nice than what's actually right, dear. Now, be a good boy and throw some of these other books away.'

*　　　*　　　*

In the evening Helen went home, and Guy fetched a Chinese take-out from Kirksfield. After we had eaten, I sat at the table with my mum and dad watching television, while Guy went out to replace a punctured tyre on the Fourtrak. After twenty minutes he returned to the kitchen and asked me if I was busy, and then took me outside to show me the flint that had punctured the tyre. It was as big as his fist, with jagged edges and a dull glitter under its surface. A daft thing to have called me to come and look at, but still something you would like someone to see.

'It's a lovely stone, flint,' I said. 'With the light on it. You know.'

'Here,' he said, holding it out. 'You can have it if you want.'

'I don't know what I'd do with it.'

'Could you use it as a paperweight?'

I took it from his hand. We stood in silence for a moment, and he looked up at the clear night sky. 'Frosty tomorrow morning,' he said.

By half past ten I was alone in the sitting room downstairs, and all was quiet except for the hapless miaow of confused cats, the steel ticking of the radiators and the church clock opposite striking the late quarter hours. There were no curtains, and I could see the room reflected in the darkness outside. On the walls there were grubby outlines of grime where pictures of horses and olde worlde farmyards had hung, and on the floor a rectangle of fluff where the bookcase used to stand. A patch of carpet was worn threadbare where my dad's feet had rubbed in front of his chair, in which he sat every day after going out to feed up—sitting down to watch a Western then falling asleep amid the stampedes and gunshots.

Guy came downstairs and we watched football highlights together.

'Wonder what they'll call it when it's all gone,' he said.

'Maybe it'll be named after you, like Guy Street, or Guy Road, or something.'

'Oh, I very much doubt they'll use "road" or "street".'

I laughed.

'I'm not joking. Modern streets are called

208

"paddock" or "field" or summat, aren't they? After what they were built on top of.'

'I suppose there are more new streets around here than there are in London,' I replied, but he wasn't really listening.

To my surprise, he said, 'This is the last time we'll sleep in this house, in't it, Rich?'

I asked him if that made him feel sad, and he gruffly conceded that it did. We talked about the model farm we built on a table in his bedroom, and how it grew so big we had to move it down on to the floor, where it expanded to fill the whole room. He blinked and swallowed. To change the subject, I asked him what his five happiest memories were. For a long time he didn't say anything. He looked as if he'd been asked for the answer to the maths problem he'd been working on all his life, but didn't have it to give. 'Can't think,' he said eventually. 'My mind doesn't seem to work like that.'

Peter Rabbit Has Left the Building

The next day we carted the rest of the furniture from the house up to the spinney, and Mr Martin called to collect the keys. After the first night in the caravans we woke up to the sound of a hard, full rain beating on the metal roofs. The wall of bales behind us could not hold back the wind, and when I opened the thin aluminium door, gusts pushed it back. I pushed harder, until the wind grabbed hold and flung the door flat open. In front of the caravans and the wooden hut was a thirty-foot-square patch of land, once used for haystacks, that was where the house was to be built; to one side were trees, and to another was rough earth with trenches dug into it for the caravans' plumbing. On all the ground water stood in muddy pools, and a dense fog had reduced visibility to about fifty feet.

'Morning!' said my mum, splashing across to the hut with a box of kitchen utensils. 'Exciting, in't it?'

We spent the day unpacking, and at five o'clock I went with my dad to fetch the rabbit and the rest of the stuff from the outhouse. It was already early dusk as we rode down into the village on the tractor. When we reached the house there was a red Toyota Landcruiser parked at the bottom of the garden, and a light on in the kitchen.

I knocked on the door, and Mr Martin shouted for us to come in. He sounded personable and easygoing, in a sort of modern, confident way. I stepped into the hallway and my dad lingered at the doorstep, and we all made small talk and jokes until we ran out of ready subjects. Then Mr Martin sympathetically, and perhaps a little curiously, said, 'This must be very strange for you, Gordon.'

'Aye, well,' my dad said, and pulled at the brim of his cap. They talked a little more, Mr Martin with his arms folded, leaning on the wall, and my dad tugging the hem of his padded overshirt and occasionally squeezing the bridge of his nose between thumb and forefinger.

Then Mr Martin made a game attempt to round off the conversation by remarking that the wet weather had not helped, and suddenly my dad looked up like a gundog scenting grouse. He took

210

a short, preparatory sigh. 'Aye,' he said. 'We've had some rain, haven't we?'

But Mr Martin was as yet unused to Sowthistle conversations about the weather and, I thought, with a defensive reflex that took me rather by surprise, perhaps not yet aware that when people here talked about the rain, they were sometimes talking not just about meteorology, but also, in code, about the places that they loved. 'Oh yes,' he said, taking a deep, conclusive breath. *'Anyway—'*

'Yes, we shall have to sort this rabbit out,' said my dad.

'Yes, I'll let you get on with the dinner!' replied Mr Martin, and we all laughed.

We packed and carried boxes for about two hours until, finally, it was Peter's turn. My dad put his hand in the hutch, pulled the rabbit out and held him close, with one hand underneath and another stroking his ears. I carried the hutch down the path and put it in the trailer, with Dad following, shushing the wriggling ball of fur.

Two boys of about eight or nine were dawdling under the lamplight, looking at the tractor and measuring themselves against the size of the wheels. They glanced up at us, and then craned to look into my dad's hands.

'It's a rabbit,' I offered helpfully.

'We know,' one of them said.

They moved forward with their right arms outstretched, and the other one said, 'Can we stroke it?'

'Aye, gentle though—'

As the fine rain swirled around us all golden-orange under the light, Dad lowered his arms and the children laid their small white hands on the

211

rabbit's back. Peter seemed to enjoy it for a while, but then began twitching in preparation for a leap.

'Come on then, it's time for him to go now,' he said. They stood aside as he straightened his back, turned, slipped Peter into the hutch and slid the bolt. He closed the trailer door, leaving the two boys watching on the pavement as we drove away.

At the Monument

The next morning we set about adding some homely, civilized touches to the encampment. Ignoring the squally wind and rain, Guy clambered over the caravans trying to attach television aerials to their roofs, while Dad laid down flagstones across the surrounding mud swamps. My mother sent me to Kirksfield to buy extension cables, buckets and other small items such as you find you need when relocating to two static caravans and a wooden hut.

By the time I had done the shopping and set off back from Kirksfield, the rain had stopped, and in the cold, clear light the countryside looked immaculate and wild. On an impulse, I turned off the road and drove up the hill to the Skelton Monument. I parked, and stood beneath a stone frieze showing Sir Chester on a horse, both man and animal staring out quizzically over the Wolds. Following their gazes across the hills and the flat land to the east, I wondered what the landscape would be like when I had been dead for as long as Sir Chester. Covered with houses? A cereal prairie shared between half a dozen growers? A patchwork of small branded fields containing speciality crops and livestock? Perhaps there would be rural theme parks, or vast off-roading tracks, or landscaped gardens. These seemed strange ideas, but then the idea of the fields that were there now would have seemed strange to people before the enclosures.

Would there be new work and businesses to employ the people in the landscape, or would they all work in cities and motorway-junction towns? Would all villages like Sowthistle be long-range suburbs?

Regardless of what Guy had said when we argued, I felt that there in that landscape something good and valuable was being lost. I remembered Mal saying he didn't know what would happen to silly old buggers like him, and then for some reason I recalled the speech about glistening bulls at Stuart's funeral, and then I thought about Stuart, whose death seemed at that moment like a death from loneliness, the great, secret disease of a new world in which everyone had grown too far apart.

I had lost track of how long I had been standing there when a big Massey Ferguson tractor came down the road pulling a trailerful of potatoes. I looked up at the lad driving. He was, I guessed, in his early thirties, with gingery stubble and a back as broad and square as a kitchen table. As he drove he was singing along with the radio and slapping his thigh in time. I suddenly felt a fool standing there being miserable, but as he drove past he looked across to me, and seeing me looking back, put his hand to his brow in greeting and smiled. For a moment I wondered if he was someone I knew, but I couldn't place him. I waved back, and as he went on down the road I enjoyed the feeling of belonging to a place where random friends or friendly people hailed you cheerily from their tractor cabs.

But I knew I was kidding myself. I didn't belong there, did I? If I really belonged there, wouldn't I have been driving along singing and slapping my thigh instead of standing next to a monument on my own, being miserable? I suddenly saw that much of my regret for what was being lost was selfish. It wasn't the changing Wolds I was grieving for at all: it was myself, and the things I had lost. In the end, I was just another city person imposing a set of ideas on the countryside that the countryside had never claimed for itself.

The world was always ending and starting again. What was the point of trying to stop time? Even places themselves would become no more than ideas and memories in the end. The only places that would remain the same would be those in our imaginations. The Sowthistle on the map was not the Sowthistle in my head, and the Sowthistle in my head was not the Sowthistle in Guy's.

Not everyone's stories could have monuments to make them still points in time like the Skeltons'. In the end most of them would go into the earth or the fire with us, our lives written into the landscape or scattered as ashes on the winds until even the idea of us finally dispersed into thin air. The only hope was to be in the moment and to sing along with the music as you roared down the road.

Jim Croskill's farm was near here. The boy would have mistaken me for Guy.

214

It was time for me to go home.

Foxgloves

Over the winter I visited the caravans for a few days each month. At Christmas, Helen and I rented a cottage near Sowthistle, and the family spent Christmas Day there. Anne came to stay, and at midnight on New Year's Eve as we stood among the crowd in Kirksfield's market square she squeezed my hand and said, 'I think it's *lovely*. I don't know what you worry about sometimes.'

When the cold fogs and frosts and snows came, Mum and Dad added more straw to the wall, wrapped their mattresses in woollen blankets, and holed up in the evenings like Arctic pioneers in their foam-and-chipboard nests. In the spring Mum left the café, and on dry days Billy's father, a builder, came to dig out the foundations for the house. A pair of blackbirds built a nest in the kitchen-hut roof.

For a while I gave up my daft ideas about belonging, or reliving my childhood, or whatever it was I had been thinking about. Dad paid me back for the fork-lift, Guy met a new girlfriend and had less interest in taking me out in the Fourtrak, and I took on a new, long-term work project in London. I stopped worrying. Then, one warm evening in the early summer, a strange, small thing happened.

*   *   *

I had gone on a routine trip back to Sowthistle.

215

Mum came to York station to collect me.

'Sorry I'm late,' she said. 'I think the world's gone mad!'

'Why?'

We set off towards the car park.

'Folks dashing about everywhere! I don't know where they all come from!'

'It is a railway station, Mum.'

'Very funny. I mean on t' roads. I was stuck behind a big straw wagon all the way here, otherwise I would have been early.'

We followed another straw wagon most of the way home, caught in its blustery trail of barley stems and dust. Off the ring road, across the vale and over the hills. The Wolds were all summer sweet-shop colours, oilseed rape flowers sherbert-lemon yellow, the copper beech leaves liquorice red. Up the lane the caravans looked as if they were sinking in dog-deep grasses and cow parsley.

'We're having a thing wi' t' crows,' said my mum. 'Coming and landing on t' roof in a morning . . . it sounds like they're wearing boots. I had to make your dad get up and tell them to get off yesterday. And we had hell on last night because t' owl flew into a tree wi' two crows roosting in it and they flew out shouting and cursing him. It was pandemonium. I was eating a crumpet, and I thought they were never going to quiet down.'

At a wobbly Formica-topped table we ate bacon chops with mushroom gravy and bread from the baker's van. Then, as it was a light, dry night, my mum announced that we were going for a walk along the lane.

'Go and tell t' crows to go away,' my mum said to Jack Gemble's Jack Russell as the dog came

216

through the grass ahead of his slower and stiffer owner, and sniffed at our boots. Then, turning to me, 'They'll see him coming—they're too cute. That's why witches have them.'

'Gran' neet,' Jack began, and Dad stopped to talk weather as Mum and I walked on.

'Birds' eyes, look.' She pointed with a toe into some grasses, where there were some thin straggles of speedwell flowers. 'We used to say if you picked them, birds'd come and peck your eyes out. Same as mother-die—you know, white campion—except we said picking that killed your mum.'

'What about foxgloves, then?' There was a clump of magenta-and-white foxgloves near some elder trees where we stood waiting for my dad.

'I suppose somebody thought foxes must wear them. It sounds like something Jack'd tell you.'

'Maybe it was one of his ancestors.'

'It probably was. All these cultivated flowers you get for your garden, you know, they all come from these.' She saw my dad coming up the lane to us. 'We were just looking at t' flowers,' she said to him.

'Jack says there's a great big lump of cowslips out up at t' top of t' lane,' he said. 'We should walk up and have a look.'

I was expecting him to pass on warnings about the possibility of a freak hail storm or gale, but no: tonight all was calm, even in the mind of Jack Gemble.

*   *   *

Because the lanes of the Yorkshire Wolds are

217

broad, and because many of their slopes are too steep to cultivate, they have kept some of the wild plants that have been lost in other parts of England since the war. As we walked further up, into the less-used part of the lane, high fescues and black-and-red corn poppies came up to our knees, forget-me-nots and speedwell dotted the shorter grasses, and big white cornbine flowers sat like ivory fairy lights in the brambles. Raggy bluish-green sow-thistles stood tall, their leaves kind to the touch and delicate in the soft light.

Dad pointed out a clump of red clover to me. 'Tha dun't see so much red clover now,' he said. 'We used to put grass or clover down for a year if a field got a bit thin, tha knows, and if it were still thin after that we planted a crop of mustard and ploughed it in to put t' goodness back. Now all tha needs to do is stick some more fertilizer on. That's how it's changed, see . . .' for a moment his mind drifted back and forth across decades, and then he continued, in mixed tones of admiration and regret, 'One day last summer I watched two men come and cut a hundred-acre field of barley across from t' spinney. It took them two a single day to harvest t' whole field, and then get it drilled again. A single day, lad: it used to take us best part of a week to do fifteen acres, and that in't so long ago either. I see 'em combining in July now wi' these fast-growing varieties, and it makes me wonder if they'll have two crops off in a year eventually, and sell it all to China. That old cycle of a year, where tha sows and reaps and spends thy time preparing t' ground again—I think it'll be gone soon enough. Tha'll not work all year round, tha'll work like bloody hell for a few days and then leave it, and

218

they'll fit another season into t' year afore they've done. Nobody knows what could come wi' t' GM and that . . . and maybe there's nowt wrong wi' it changing. Who's to say, in t' end?'

'Are you reminiscing, lad?' Mum, carrying a small handful of grasses, came up alongside him and slipped her right arm through his as they walked beneath a green canopy of elders. All around them the light was tiring now, and the outlines of single black trees, plantations and the Monument grew softer. Smoky pink dabs in the sky tinted the creamy blossom and cow-parsley flowers. Mum said she had taken the grass to dry for seeds so that she could spread them down the lane, outside the caravans.

'I used to like this one when I was a kid,' said my dad, picking a stem of grass from the ground. 'Cock's foot. Can tha see why they call it that? Look—' he pushed the head of the grass against his palm to make the shape of a large bird's foot. 'I don't know why, I just used to like t' idea that it looks just like a cock's foot.'

'Well, sort of,' said my mum.

'It makes you think of a cock's foot, that's t' point.'

'You don't see as many flowers as you used to,' said Mum. 'It's a lot to do with all these sprays.'

'Mmm,' he said. 'They're doing a lot wi' conservation and t' field margins and all that now though.' Then he had another memory: 'Me and my dad had a pasture field at Marwood, and it was wick wi' flowers in t' spring and summer . . . fat hen, granny's bonnets, blobs, primrose—tha couldn't count 'em all. Ministry of Agriculture came and told us to plough it up because they were

219

short of food after t' war. They paid you six pound an acre to do it, which were a lot of money, so . . .'

We came to the clump of cowslips and stood looking down on them for a moment. Evening breezes quivered the stalks, shaking the tiny flowers into yellow clouds just above the ground. 'Milk maids, some people call them,' said Mum. 'They're supposed to grow where cows go—oh, look, Gordon!' A hare was running across a field close to the edge of the lane. Dad followed her gaze, and they both watched it as it scooted a few yards, paused to sniff at the air, and then ran onwards. And as they stood watching it, I looked from them to the flowers and then back at the plants in the lane, and I felt a strange wave of emotion breaking over me.

I cannot describe that wave, except to say that sometimes, if you stand still and look around you, you can find yourself looking at something you have looked at a million times before and suddenly see in it all the complexity and beauty of the universe. An object lying neglected on the ground can become a story, and understanding that story can make you a part of it yourself. It wasn't the beauty of the flowers that struck me standing there in the lane so much as the names; those names came from instinctively seeing stories and symbols and magic in the world around you. Billy would say that kind of relationship with the environment was dying out, and he might be right, but surely it lived on in the names of those plants?

I remembered from studying *A Midsummer Night's Dream* at school that love-in-idleness, the flower whose juice Oberon squeezed on Titania's eyes, was another name for the heartsease that grew in lanes and verges. And that Chaucer wrote about 'dayes eyes' because people thought of daisies as the eyes of the day. That folklore and poetry was still there in the landscape, living on in the words people used to describe it, if you chose to look at it that way.

That night, lying on a thin foam mattress in Guy's caravan, I slept badly. At about two in the morning, I sat up and looked out of the small window at the moonlight-lacquered lane. In a restive, insomniac way I tried to think of more flower names. And then, looking across to the patch of rough ground with the pipe-trenches in it, I had an idea.

Seeds

I asked my mum and dad if I could fill in the trenches in the rough patch of ground and then clear it so that I could sow a meadow of wild flowers and grasses. I said that I could maintain it when I visited them, and to make it seem a practical idea, I suggested that one day we could sell some of the flowers, and perhaps even install beehives to make saleable honey. Neither of them looked convinced by these commercial angles, but they both responded with a mild, if somewhat bemused, cheerfulness.

'Aye, if tha likes,' said my dad.

'I've got some heartsease in pots that you can have,' said my mum. 'I call 'em thugs, cos they take over your garden.'

I drove to Winterswick to ask Billy's advice

about seeds. 'You know you'll have to spray it all off first, don't you?' he said.

'I was going to see if I could dig all the weeds out. I just wanted to try doing it sort of . . . organic.' This was not because of a principle: I liked the idea of farmers using less chemicals, but as Guy and Billy had told me in the past, the modern global markets and profit margins made it difficult for large-scale producers to change. I just wanted to try to do things as naturally as I could, that was all. It brought the meadow more into keeping with the old practices my dad knew about.

'Weeds on disturbed ground will just out-compete whatever you put in there, old chum,' said Billy, regretfully. 'Just spray it off once, and then you should be able to look after it without any more.'

Billy had decided to move to York, although he was to carry on working in Winterswick. He told me about a meeting he had had that week with a very conservative rural conservation group. 'Some of them drive you mad in this job. They're so obsessed with preserving the past, and they don't seem to see that most of those buildings or landscapes they like came out of necessity. Old chalk barns weren't designed out of sentiment, they were an honest expression of what was needed, what we knew and what was available at the time. Chalk is a rubbish building material. People only used it because they needed shelter and it's all they had, but now it's presented as something that defines what a place is allowed to be . . .'

'You sound as if you're not going to have many

222

fond memories of it when you're done.'

He rubbed his jaw, and stared off into the middle distance for a moment. 'No, I do. It's hard not to have fond memories about places in the country because of the smells and the softness and the sounds, all the evocative sensory things about them. But I'd say that my happy memories of the countryside, especially of growing up there, are to do with my particular experiences. I'd think about driving down a back lane in East Yorkshire with my dad in his van, and stopping because he had seen someone he knew, and listening to them taking the piss out of each other. I wouldn't think of the picture-postcard images, which are images which are other people's ideas, and which bear little relation to what I see. Anyway. Time for another pickled egg, I think.'

Billy promised to e-mail me with the telephone numbers of some merchants who sold seeds to the council. I tried telling him about the names of wild flowers, and he was as sceptical as I had expected, but in the e-mail he sent me a week later he told me to avoid aggressive ryegrass because, in his opinion, it 'glistened with the sperm of Satan'.

*   *   *

'Why am I here, again?' Helen asked me. She was sitting in the passenger seat of the car as we followed a lorry carrying turkey crates along the Winterswick road one day in early September.

'Moral support,' I replied. 'Plus I didn't want to ask Guy because he'd laugh.'

'Just so long as I know,' she said, winding down the window. 'Sometimes I think I'd like to work

223

with plants.'

'I thought you wanted to work in a donkey sanctuary?'

'Donkey sanctuary first, garden centre second— I dunno. Just to not have all—' she made her hands into claws, and froze them in mid-air at her temples. '—that. Actually, sometimes I wish I could just be a dog.'

She popped a dance compilation CD from its case and pushed it into the player.

'Kids are fascinated by seeds and bulbs, you know. We grow amaryllis with them. They love seeing it grow, and it teaches them to look after things. We have a gardening club at this school I'm at now. One little kid asked me if we could grow the food for the school dinners in it.'

We passed the great sheds of the bacon factory on the Winterswick industrial estate and drove past houses, a garage and an old pottery now converted to office spaces. The agricultural trading association store was a purpose-built brick building yard opposite a Kwik Save on a strip of land between the river and the railway station. I parked in its yard, which was full of feed and animal husbandry products: chicken flint grit, bruised oats, salt blocks. A sign near the door said 'Country Store—everybody welcome'. Inside there was a sweet scent of molasses and fishmeal. Strip lights shone down on pallets of feed sacks. In one corner, a man stood behind a counter piled with small tools and record books.

'Blood powder,' said my sister, warily fingering a plastic bottle. 'Nice. I like the sound of "food for working dogs", though. That's the kind of dog you want.'

224

'I thought you might not like it here,' I said.

'No, it's interesting,' she replied. 'Are you going to get on with it and ask for something?'

'I was sort of wondering how to start, to tell you the truth.'

'How about: "Hello, I am from the town. I would like to buy some seeds"?'

'Thanks.'

The man behind the counter was in his sixties, bearded and benign-looking. He wore a blue smocky jacket, had rheumy eyes and spoke softly.

'Um, do you sell seeds?' I said. Helen covered her mouth with her hand.

'What kind?'

'Grass, but what I wanted was a mix with some flowers. I want to make a mea—'

'A meadow?' he said. 'We have mixes we can order for you.'

'Do you not do your own?'

'No, we don't do our own seeds any more,' he said. 'Rules and regulations are that tight it's got too expensive to clean 'em.'

He pulled from under his counter a glossy A5 catalogue with an Advanta Seeds logo on the front.

'There's a lot of meadows being planted with the stewardship schemes now, you see,' he said.

'Right,' I said.

Helen flipped through the catalogue, which was full of idyllic scenes in which men in overalls and baseball caps emptied seeds into large drills. 'Look at the names of the grasses!' she said to the man. I hadn't told her what I thought about the flower names. 'Crested dog's-tail . . . chewings fescue . . . don't you think they're good?'

'Oh aye, there're some funny ones,' he said. 'Er,

225

do you want to take it and have a look and then come and let me know?'

* * *

Advanta, as I found out from looking on the Internet, was a multinational corporation that had recently sold European farmers some GM-contaminated oilseed rape seed by accident. This didn't exactly feel like the sort of company I wanted to buy seeds from, so I started again.

'You could just try rough mix,' said my dad, when I asked him what he thought one night in the caravan. 'Farmways should sell it. Make sure you put plenty on, that's the thing.'

'Maybe we could order some on the Internet,' I said.

'Can you do that?'

'I would have thought you could,' I said.

'You could get them off a gardening site,' said my mum, without taking her eyes off the Western playing on the video.

Me and my dad turned and looked at her, and she looked back.

'There's loads of them. Silver surfers go on 'em.'

The following Saturday I drove to a wildflower farm in Nottinghamshire that I had discovered using Google.

Happiness

'What would you have done if you hadn't done farming?' I asked Guy one night as we were watching television in the caravan.

'Dunno, really. What would you have done if you'd had a proper job?'

'Very funny. I don't know either.' I did know, but I felt a bit stupid saying it. 'Um, sometimes I think I would've liked being a zoologist, though.'

He looked up, bemused. 'But you don't even like animals.'

'Yes I do. Just because I wasn't any good at looking after them doesn't mean I didn't like them, does it?'

'No, I suppose not,' he said uninterestedly, and switched his attention back to *The Simpsons*.

'Do you remember that summer when all those pigs got meningitis?' I asked.

'Aye, when they all went round wi' their heads like this—?'

'Yes. Do you remember we had some in a little pen in the barn?'

He raised his eyebrows quite high for about three seconds, indicating a thorough search of his memory and said, 'No, I don't remember. Why?'

'It doesn't matter.'

Bart stole a doughnut. Guy reached for a ham sandwich.

'Do you remember when your cat caught that blackbird?'

'Eh?' he said, through a mouthful of meat and bread.

227

'One of your cats caught a blackbird, and you were upset about it. You'd be about sixteen.'

He raised his eyebrows again, and shook his head. 'No . . . I remember there being a blackbird down t' yard, but I don't remember a cat killing one.'

'Never mind.' He seemed quite amenable to being asked questions tonight, so I asked him another, more difficult one. 'Would you say you were happy, Guy?'

'No, I don't have time to be happy, lad,' he said, in his *Power Farming* voice. When I didn't say anything back, he sighed, had another bite of his sandwich and, because he guessed that I had expected a joke, now gave the issue some thought. 'I don't know,' he said. 'It's hard to say if you're really happy, in't it? Like, are you happy if you're just doing all right, or do you have to be all ooh-I-love-my-life? I'd say I'm happy when I'm wi' t' bullocks at Jim's. But summat always happens, dun't it? You're not ever actually going to be properly happy for more than ten minutes, when you think about it.'

'Ten minutes is a bit grim.'

'Maybe half an hour, then. How's plans for your flower patch coming on, anyway?'

'All right, thank you. And don't laugh when you ask me that, please.'

'Why did you think I was laughing?'

'You called it a flower patch. It's going to be a meadow.'

'Fucks's sake,' he said. 'Meadow, then.'

'Maybe we could make honey off the flowers. Organic, or something.'

'Calm down,' he said. 'Mind you, Gerald
228

Thwaites is supposed to be going organic, you know. I hope you make it grow, anyway.'

'Do you?'

'Of course I do, you fucking idiot.'

'Thank you, Guy.'

'That's all right, brother,' he said.

The Meadow

I had to admit that the bit of land, tangled with knotgrass, nettles, thistles and cleavers, looked a lot more like neglected urban scrub than a potential meadow. All the plants were dying off, dropping their seeds into the soil for next year, and once the first flush of my idea had gone, I began to feel slightly ridiculous.

One day in September I took a strimmer, hoe, spade and fork into a patch of uneven, stony soil and began trying to clear it. I dug up all the flowers that were scattered about in the thick, creeping weeds and replanted them in the patches where clover had kept the knotgrass at bay. Next I began removing the thistles and pulling out long skeins of cornbine and cleavers, and dead stalks of docks and cow parsley. The long grass was black and dead on top and yellow and damp beneath. The knotgrass and couch-grass roots were tough, and I saw why my dad called them ironweed and twitch. I bent down to try pulling them up by hand and got thistle needles through my gloves. I tried forking them out, but on Wolds hillsides the topsoil is thin, with a layer of chalk only an inch below the surface, and it was hard to get down to the roots.

By the afternoon of the second day I had cleared only about eight square feet, and felt frustrated. The sun hung low in the sky and the light was hard and bright. It had been dry for a long time, and so when the soil was uncovered it blew into my eyes. My dad came over and said, non-commitally, 'We could just spray 'em off once to get rid of 'em, tha knows.'

'I'd rather not.'

'All right,' he said. He stood looking a bit, and then walked away, back into the shed he had been working in.

For a moment I imagined him reappearing with a fork or a hoe and falling to beside me, in a comradely way, but then I heard steely scrapes and ringings from the shed, which meant he had begun tinkering with another job. In the end, then, he thought it was a daft idea—worth humouring me for, but . . . Well, maybe it was a daft idea. After all, I didn't really know what the point was myself.

The sun was cold and glaring. I carried on jabbing and digging, and the patch of bare earth widened by inches, while the pile of uprooted grass, cleavers and cornbine grew taller, and dried in the sun like weedy, useless autumn hay. I wished Guy was there to help, but he had taken his girlfriend out to Bridlington. From the corner of my eye I saw something in the soil twitching a couple of feet away, and went to look: it was a black toad, about the size of my palm and all dusted with soil. I must have pulled away his cover, because now he was laboriously scrambling over the disturbed ground looking for somewhere to hide. He looked up at me, and I looked back at him, apologetically. I wondered if I shouldn't just give up.

I laid the spade down on the grass pile, and wiped the sweat from my brow and eyes. Crows called, my dad's hammer rang, and my mum talked to the cat as she hung washing on a line tied to the shipping container. The cleared patch was still tiny. I raked off some of the chalk and flint, tipping it on a little mound next to the weed-hay, but that felt even more pointless.

Then Jack Gemble's dog scuttled by, with Jack lumbering along after it. Please don't say anything sarcastic, I thought.

'Now, lad,' he said.

'Now, Jack.' Here it came.

'Grand day.' No, maybe not! Good. Good!

'Oh, aye.'

'Has 'e got tha gardenin' then?' I thought he might have snickered, but I wasn't sure.

'Something like that,' I said, and fell back to picking up the stones before he asked if gardenin' was a bit different to whatever it was I did in London.

'Tha wants to make on while this weather holds up,' he said. 'We shall pay for it come t' winter.'

'So I hear.'

'There's some young foxes up there,' he said. 'Have you seen 'em? They're smashing.'

We regarded each other impassively for a few seconds, and then suddenly at the top of the lane there was the snarl of diesel engines. Turning into it was a short procession of four-by-fours: two Land-Rovers, a Nissan and an Isuzu. Gemble gathered his dog and shrank himself right up into the hedge. They bounced by in a cloud of noise and blue smoke.

'Bloody hell,' he said as we stared after them. 'It's getting to be like an amusement park up this lane.'

'Well, I'd better get on, Jack,' I said.

'Aye.'

'So.'

'Aye.'

Pause.

'It'll be making thy bloody back ache a bit!' he said.

I looked at him. He was smiling underneath his cap.

'It bloody does,' I said.

'Aye,' he said.

We stood there in silence, hearing the diesel engines dying away up the road. The wind moved some grass. Gemble's dog came nudging at his ankles and the old man bent down to pick him up.

'My dog's badly,' he said. I noticed the Jack Russell was limping. He must have been about fourteen. 'I shall have to take him to t' vet.' He looked at me as a drowning man might look at someone on a shore who was too far away to save him.

'Vet'll know if there's anything he can do for him, Jack,' I said. 'It's best place.'

Then there was a long silence between us. 'Aye,' he said. 'Aye, well. I shall have to be moving on.'

'Aye,' I said.

'Soon be winter.'

*   *   *

I was emptying another basket of stones when I heard the sound of an engine coming from the

232

shed. I turned to look. The hammering noise had been my dad putting the big bucket on the front of the fork-lift. He drove it up to the edge of the rough ground and, leaning out of the window, shouted over the noise of the diesel engine.

'Does tha just want it levelling off, and all t' weeds taking off t' top?'

'Yes please!' I shouted back.

He coaxed the fork-lift back and forth, tweaking the levers to make fractional up and down adjustments to the bucket, so that it skimmed off the surface layer of the ground and brought up the weeds' roots. It took ten minutes to clear the whole patch. He leaned out again, grinning: 'Is that all right for thee?'

'Not bad,' I said, and smiled—both at him, and at the pleasure of watching a well-handled machine do in ten minutes a job which would otherwise have taken hours. He puttered off, and I took the spade and levelled off the soil. Then I took a rake and pulled off the weeds and grass still lying on top, and the lumps of chalk and flint that lay on the surface.

I was going back to London that night, but there would still be enough time to sow some of the seeds. It was mid-afternoon when I took two polythene storage tubs and poured into one of them the grass seed and into the other all the flower seeds: the tufted darts of cornflower, the dust of speedwell, the wheaty pods of field scabious. When I tipped in the last yellow envelope, chuting tiny, pale-green, rounded points of ox-eye daisy into the container, I swirled the tub to mix them and then looked at them for a minute. And then I knew what I wanted to do. Measuring

233

one part of flowers to four of grass, I poured the flower seeds into the grasses and stirred and stirred until they were all mingled together. Then I put a lid on the container and went to the shed. My dad was putting the tines back on the fork-lift.

'Look,' I said, and held up the container.

He took it from me and looked. He removed the top delicately, and pulled out some seeds and let them run through his fingers. 'Mmm,' he said. 'It looks all right.'

'Will you help me put it on?'

He grinned and looked diffident. 'Tha just gets some in thy fingers—' he put his finger and thumb together and turned his hand upwards '—and then tha's to spread it over, say, a yard as even as tha can. Tha must try to spread it even.'

I mimed copying him. 'I suppose I can have a go.' I didn't move, and looked away over the landscape.

'Is tha all right doing it?'

'I suppose I'll manage. I might waste a bit.'

I saw a flicker cross his face. 'Have a go and see how tha gets on.'

'OK,' I said, and walked off slowly towards the ground.

He came over before I'd thrown anything, and toed the soil with his boot. 'Tha's got that looking grand,' he said, looking down and studying. 'That's how we used to like to get it. Does tha want me to show thee how to do them seeds?'

I took the lid off the tub and held it out, and the wind lifted a fine dust off the top.

He reached underneath into the pot and took a pinch of the dust, and as we stood in the greying brown, dry soil laced with flint and chalk, he said,

234

'Tha just goes like—' and with a weirdly delicate motion, he flung it down and crossways at the earth. I saw the grains leave his fingertips in a tiny parabola, and melt away into the light, and then I tried it: it felt like a strangely small movement.

'That's it, just spread it,' he said. 'Main thing is to watch where tha's been. That's why when tha does a field tha's to time thy walk wi' how tha spreads it. I used to do one stride to one throw, but tha'd to get thy hand back to thy seed for the next 'un. My grandad had a right knack for it, tha knows. He used to come and do my dad's fields right up until he died. He used to get a washing-up bowl full of seed under his left arm and walk like that, one stride to one throw. My dad, thy grandad, could never do it.'

'How do you mean?'

'He just couldn't do it. He couldn't time his stride to his throw. He used to get one and a half strides in. He tried and tried wi' it, but he never could just get the hang of it. When his dad died, I started doing it. He never figured it out, like. Just couldn't, somehow.'

'Oh,' I said.

'When we got a fiddle drill I used to go and do it for other folks. I used to go and start at four o'clock in t' morning, walking up and down fields like bloody hell. I walked miles before anybody were up, galloping up and down at five shilling an acre. It wasn't owt unusual like, that's how folks used to work in those days. Too hard, looking back.'

And then there was a hush on the hillside, and I experienced a strange sense of calmness that I have never quite forgotten. To this day I can sit at

235

a desk writing, as I am doing now, and recall exactly the feeling of being there that afternoon, see again the two of us standing on the patch of ground, feel the temperature of the air against my face. There is the sound of the wind in the trees, Jack Gemble calls to his dog, and a solitary crow caws as it passes above our heads.

'There's some grand plants in t' hedge there, look,' says my dad.

Foxgloves, whose flowers are worn by foxes, and whose leaves can cure your heart. Cornflowers, campion and celandine to soothe your dreams.

'Bacon-and-eggs,' he says, picking at a bit of bird's-foot trefoil. 'There used to be no end of that in t' pasture at Marwood . . . anyroad, come and walk wi' me, and watch where tha's been, and hope that t' birds don't find t' seed.' I scoop up some seeds in my left hand so that I can throw them out with my right, and he stands three yards to the side of me so that he can do the same. We start walking forward, one stride to one throw, across the ground where we laid out the gates for selling.

Meadowgrass, speedwell, cowslip and foxglove; dog rose, cock's foot, clover and heartsease. The October sun casts our shadows on the earth beside us. We walk across the waste ground together, scattering seeds into the early autumn wind.

Epilogue

At the time of writing my mum and dad had almost completed their new house. My dad says he knows he ought to retire, but he hates the idea and continues to sell straw bales. Helen is still a teacher in Hull, and continues to dream of running a donkey sanctuary. Guy still works mostly for Jim Croskill, and has a new truck, a Mitsubishi L200 pick-up, which he keeps cleaner than the old Fourtrak.

Mal still has his farm, Karl still works on the farm near York, and Jack Gemble still walks along the lane in Sowthistle. Major and Mrs Twist say they miss the pigs.

Billy now lives in York with his partner. Mr and Mrs Martin and my mum and dad have become firm friends.

Peter Rabbit died peacefully in his sleep as I was writing this book. Double and Trouble enjoy a happy retirement in the sheds. One of the two farm cats disappeared, presumed taken by the fox or accidentally shot in the lane by lampers. Jack Gemble's dog made a full recovery.

Weeds grew back and smothered the first seeds we sowed on the rough ground, and so I used a glyphosate herbicide to kill them off, and sowed some more.

*   *   *

In 1939 there were 500,000 farms in Britain, including part-time holdings. The majority of these farms were small mixed units of less than 50 acres, and one and half million families made their living directly from agriculture. There are now 191,000 farms left, and of those 19,000 account for more than 50 per cent of national output. It is estimated that three out of four jobs in British agriculture have been lost since 1945.

The Common Agricultural Policy costs British people £6.5bn annually. Since the scheme's inception, across the European Union 17 per cent of farms have received over 50 per cent of the subsidies provided by the CAP. In 2002, 87 per cent of respondents to a survey of British farmers conducted by the farmers' organization FARM said they would prefer to operate in a subsidy-free market.

Two international grain traders—Cargill and Archer Daniels Midlands—control approximately 80 per cent of the world's grain trade. Six companies—BASF, Bayer, Dow, Dupont, Monsanto and Syngenta—control almost 70 per cent of global pesticide sales. Four companies— Tesco, Asda-Walmart, Sainsbury's and Morrison's —control more than 70 per cent of grocery sales in the UK. British farmers receive, on average, 7.5p out of every £1 spent on food in Britain. Fifty years ago the comparable figure was 50p.

Within the EU there is provision for government assistance to help people enter farming. The EU scheme assists between 24,000 and 31,000 new farmers to 'install' every year. France accounts for 40 per cent of the scheme's take-up. The UK accounts for 0 (zero) per cent.

CHIVERS
LARGE PRINT
–direct–

If you have enjoyed this Large Print book
and would like to build up your own
collection of Large Print books, please
contact

Chivers Large Print Direct

Chivers Large Print Direct offers you
a full service:

- Prompt mail order service
- Easy-to-read type
- The very best authors
- Special low prices

For further details either call
Customer Services on (01225) 336552
or write to us at Chivers Large Print Direct,
FREEPOST, Bath BA1 3ZZ

Telephone Orders:
FREEPHONE 08081 72 74 75